MASTERING THE BUSINESS INTERVIEW

Discover the keys to successful interviewing,
and turn every interview into an opportunity to
show why *you* are the best candidate for the job!

Mastering the Business Interview
is the total executive guide to
all aspects of the interview process.
You'll find invaluable information on:

- Standard interview procedures
- Interview etiquette
- Dressing for success
- Body language and your image
- Handling difficult questions
- Assessing your strengths and weaknesses
- Making yourself visible
- Fielding off-limit questions
- Protocol for restaurant interviews
- Guiding a conversation effectively
- Negotiating a salary
- Mastering media interviews
- Evaluating a job offer
  . . . AND MUCH MORE!

THE TOTAL MANAGEMENT PROGRAM FOR THE 1990s!
From the National Institute of Business Management

THIS REMARKABLE NEW SERIES INCLUDES:

MASTERING MEETINGS
MASTERING OFFICE POLITICS
MASTERING DECISION MAKING
MASTERING BUSINESS WRITING
MASTERING BUSINESS STYLE
MASTERING THE BUSINESS INTERVIEW

MASTERING
THE
BUSINESS INTERVIEW

SUCCESS STRATEGIES THAT
PUT YOU AHEAD

National Institute of Business Management

BERKLEY BOOKS, NEW YORK

MASTERING THE BUSINESS INTERVIEW

A Berkley Book / published by arrangement with
National Institute of Business Management, Inc.

PRINTING HISTORY
Berkley trade paperback edition / May 1992

ISBN: 0-425-13188-2

A BERKLEY BOOK ® TM 757,375
Berkley Books are published by The Berkley Publishing Group,
200 Madison Avenue, New York, New York 10016.
The name "BERKLEY" and the "B" logo
are trademarks belonging to Berkley Publishing Corporation.

PRINTED IN THE UNITED STATES OF AMERICA

10 9 8 7 6 5 4 3 2 1

CONTENTS

II. MASTERING MEDIA INTERVIEWS

Introduction

"If only I'd said what I should have said when I should have said it." Those words of regret have crossed everyone's mind more than once. Sometimes the missed opportunity is simply an irritant. If you didn't think quickly enough to fire off a good one to a surly clerk or cab driver, probably you suffered nothing more than a wounded ego. But if you weren't able to come up with the right words at the right time in a business conversation—a business *interview*—and therefore could not use the meeting to your best advantage, the cost was much higher. Consider . . .

• You're sitting across the desk from the vice president of sales at XYZ Company. You know that you could be the best director of training that company has ever seen, and you're counting on being offered the job. Then the vice president asks a question that takes you by surprise. You respond, "Well, I really haven't thought too much about that one. But . . ."

- You've heard that one of the best ways to find a job is through networking. But for some reason the people you know have never offered you any kind of job, good or otherwise, or even told you about an opening.

- Your company is having great success with its quality-control program, and a reporter from the local newspaper calls to ask you about it. You answer the questions on the spot, only to realize later that you completely forgot to mention several key points. When the newspaper article appears, your statements are accurate—but woefully inadequate.

Your 20–20 hindsight tells you that every one of those disasters could have been *prevented* if you had been better *prepared*. That's what this book is about: *preventing* disaster by *preparing* for success. Although damage control may be necessary on occasion, as a way of life it is distinctly deficient. You want to get it right the first time. This book will show you how.

Section I: Mastering Job Interviews

Competition for jobs keeps getting tougher. An employment ad in *The New York Times* can prompt a thousand responses. American Airlines receives half a million resumes per year. Fast-food chain Pizza Hut had eleven hundred applicants for eleven jobs when it opened an outlet in the Boston area recently. If you're going to beat out that kind of competition, you have to be smarter, faster, sharper—*better!*

In Section I, you'll find dozens of techniques, ideas, and suggestions for beating out the competition. Among them:

- How to identify, and get through to, the person who has the power to hire you
- How to work with search firms
- How to write a cover letter that stands out from the crowd
- How to respond to interviewers' hidden questions
- How to conduct the kind of networking interviews that provide solid information and that can eventually lead to job interviews
- The most common interview errors—and how to avoid them
- How to field off-limits questions
- How to handle objections
- How to answer "killer" questions
- How to keep on presenting your qualifications even after the interview is over

Even if you've been through the interview process many times, you'll find new ideas for enhancing your effectiveness. You'll benefit even more if you're a novice—if you're a recent graduate or have been with the same employer for many years and have no recent job-hunting experience.

Section II: Mastering Media Interviews

Here you'll find tips for making the most of the opportunity to be interviewed by the media. Whether you're aiming to promote your company's achievements or your own expertise, media interviews can help you reach a wide audience at little or no cost. But, just as with a job interview, you'll flub the opportunity if you're not prepared.

Some of the preparation tips in this section:

- How to avoid an ambush
- How to guarantee that you communicate your major idea
- How to build bridges that only you can cross
- How to answer "killer" questions (They're asked in media interviews as well as job interviews.)
- How to build relationships with print journalists
- How to survive crisis interviews

Many of the ideas in this book were graciously shared by experts in their fields—outplacement consultants, corporate and executive recruiters, career consultants, and specialists in image development, business protocol, and media training. The result is a practical, experience-based handbook. Following the suggestions in it will help you to improve your skills—thus greatly increasing the likelihood that you will get what you're after in today's leaner business environment.

I

MASTERING
JOB INTERVIEWS

1

Get Ready
to Start

Once upon a time (yes, this is a fairy tale), all you needed to get a good job was strong skills and solid experience. Employers would clamor for your services, and you would have your pick of several desirable jobs.

Even without the skills and experience, you might have stood a chance if you had the right attitude. A recently retired vice president of a major book publishing company recalls one of her first job interviews, thirty-plus years ago: "The interviewer asked me if I thought I could handle this job, and I said I really didn't know, because I had never done anything like this before, but I would certainly try. So he hired me."

Today, that's fantasyland. Job hunting is hard work, and getting a job is chancey, no matter how well qualified you are. And it's not just because there are fewer jobs and a greater number of skilled people competing for them—though those two factors are hardly insignificant. What makes it even more difficult is that people are better at *job hunting* than they used to be. "People have been trained to be job hunters, so anyone who has not been trained is at a disadvantage," says Executive Coach Kate Wendleton, who heads both the Career Development Program at the New School for Social Research and The Five O'Clock Club, an executive coaching and support group, both in New York City.

For example, corporations are increasingly arranging for outplacement services for employees who are let go as a result of restructuring and cost cutting. Such services teach people to be crackerjack job-seekers. And those whose employers have not provided outplacement are turning to various types of career counselors and coaches on their own, recognizing that they need all the help they can get.

Moreover, says Wendleton, "Employers are also more polished, more sophisticated, and do more digging in interviews." Although there are still some interviewers who are ill-prepared or vague even in their own minds about what they want to find out, many ask tough questions designed to unearth your deepest professional secrets. And their evaluations use criteria that go far beyond mere professional competence.

All of which means that if you hope to outshine the competition when you look for a job, you must hone your job search skills as well as your professional skills. How? This book will tell you.

The revolution in the workplace

It's a cliché that you should be looking for your next job while still working at your current one. But no one ever said clichés weren't true. And today there's more truth than ever in that one, as employer loyalty increasingly becomes a thing of the past. Not that companies don't want to keep people on board long enough to earn their gold watches. But economic realities and competitive environments make it necessary for companies to "streamline," "downsize," "flatten the pyramid into a pancake," or whatever other euphemism your company uses that makes you feel not one whit better.

Spending your days paralyzed by the fear that you may lose your job, and having no idea what you'll do if that happens, is certainly unproductive. But so is gliding along unperturbed, naively assuming that your job must be secure. After all, you've been there since the day the company opened its doors—which proves how highly you're valued. Or you know of the lowest-cost supplier for widget gaskets; the company could never get along without you. Or your cousin's brother-in-law is the company president's lodge partner, so you really have a solid connection. To use the vernacular—Get real. None of this matters anymore.

Hard work won't save you, either. A civil engineer who lost his job during a layoff protested to his supervisor, "I give you an honest day's work for a day's pay. There are guys here who are really ripping you off—they take two hours for lunch, or disappear at three o'clock on a Friday afternoon, or spend half their time drinking coffee and shooting the breeze." The supervisor's response? "But some of these guys have been with the company for twenty years!" In other words, it was last hired, first fired, regardless of dedication or contribution to the company.

Face it: Nothing—*nothing*—can protect you except your own preparedness. Then, if the ax should fall, you may be stunned, but you won't be immobilized. You will already have laid the groundwork and will be ready to start to look for a job.

But regardless of what your career situation is—employed, unemployed, or uncertain—looking for a new job is by no means a single step. Long before you face an interviewer or even schedule an interview, before you respond to an ad or talk with a search firm, before you even think about starting to look, you need to get yourself ready to start.

There are four parts to this process:

- Analyze your abilities and goals.
- Identify the opportunities for using those abilities and meeting those goals.
- Sharpen your self-marketing tools.
- Activate your network.

Analyze your abilities and goals

What kind of job would be most satisfying for you? If you don't know what you want, you won't know how to look for it—and you may not even recognize it when you find it. Ask yourself questions like these:

- ***What are my professional abilities?***
  - What am I good at?
  - What do I like to do?

These two aren't necessarily the same. You may be asked to handle an assignment that you find mind-numbing, but carry it off brilliantly because you believe in doing the best possible job regardless of what it is. It's important to maintain your self-awareness so you can make the distinction.

- What can't I do? Does it matter? Do I need to learn it in order to move ahead?
- What do I hate to do? Can I get a job that I would enjoy that doesn't require it?

A range of abilities makes you more valuable to your present employer and increases your options when you do decide to look for another job. "Don't be slotted within your own company," urges Joan Learn, president of The Greenwich Group, a Greenwich, Connecticut, outplacement firm. "Be constantly looking around, learning different functions, and upgrading your skills." That's a major message for employees who have been dismissed. She says: "They should try not to let what happened to them ever happen again."

- ***What are my professional goals?***
  - Do I want to stay in my present industry or profession, or would I like to move eventually—perhaps even now?
  - What type of position, or title, would I like to have?
  - Do I require a job that would be a step up? Or would I prefer—or be willing to make—a lateral move that would diversify my experience, making me a stronger candidate for advancement later, or perhaps putting me into an area with greater growth potential?
  - Are income and position my major concerns, or would I prefer a job that might pay less and perhaps have a less impressive title, but that would leave me more time for my family and the outside interests that are important to me?

- ***What are my preferred working conditions?***
  - What geographical location do I prefer—the one I

have? A different neighborhood in my present city? A different city? A different state?

- What kind of workplace environment do I prefer—serious and button-down, or relaxed and informal?

Observation: These are not frivolous concerns. Environmental psychologists tell us that physical surroundings have an impact on people's attitudes and thus their performance. Be aware of what conditions enable you to do your best possible work.

- Do I prefer to work in a large company, where there may be greater opportunities for advancement? Or is it more important for me to work in a small company, which might be less impersonal and where there might be more camaraderie?

Recommendation: Use your answers to these questions to create a picture of your ideal job. Yes, this exercise is a little like saying, "Here's what I want to be when I grow up." But now that you are grown up, you have the power to look for exactly what you want. Then, when you begin the actual job-search process, you can revise your requirements if you must.

Identify the opportunities

Now that you've begun to determine what kinds of jobs appeal to you, you need to look for the fields, and the companies within those fields, that might offer such jobs. Companies are constantly coming to your attention through your reading and in conversations. It's important to keep your information current by reading both general business publications and industry-specific publications, and by joining industry associations. Keep your antennae up for clues to companies that you want to learn more about.

These are some of the things that you should try to find out:

- Which companies in your field—or in another field that interests you—have a good reputation?
- Which ones handle the kind of work that you might like to do?
- Which ones have recently acquired a new project or new account?
- Which ones are hiring?
- What jobs are available? Are there many openings, or just a few?
- What skills are needed?
- Have any companies that interest you rented more space (a sign that they might be expanding) or better-quality space (a sign that their balance sheet is strong)?

Look in your own backyard. If you are thinking about a job change while you're still employed, don't neglect the possibilities within your present company. Apply your list of criteria here, as well as elsewhere. People often overlook their own companies just because they feel stymied in their particular departments, cautions Donald Allerton, president of the Chicago-based executive recruiting firm Allerton, Heinze & Associates. But many companies are large and diverse enough to provide many opportunities, especially for people who are eager to acquire more than one specialty.

IBM is one such company. "We fill our managerial

positions from within the company as exclusively as possible," says George Morgenroth, program manager, employment and recruiting, for IBM United States, Purchase, New York. One of the major advantages of such a system, Morgenroth points out, is that "we already know the person's work history. We have informal assessments going on at all times, so we're not shooting in the dark." Another plus is that an individual who has been with the company for some time knows the company culture and requires less orientation.

Such factors might work to your advantage within your own company, and make you more desirable than someone from the outside. From your perspective, too, a move within your own company requires less readjustment.

To keep up with what's happening in your company, read the annual report, of course, but also the employee newsletters. Pay attention to interoffice memos, which people so often give just a cursory glance. Have lunch or play golf with peers in other departments. Attend company functions. Be alert to remarks you overhear— don't leap to conclusions, but keep the various tidbits in your mental file until they all begin to fit together.

Sharpen your self-marketing tools

When you look for a job, you are, in effect, marketing yourself. In addition to strengthening your professional skills, you should be constantly developing and refining your marketing tools so that they are ready when you need them.

These are the basic marketing tools that will help you present yourself most effectively:

Resume
There are two reasons to keep your resume current, whether you are looking for a job or not:

- *If an unexpected opportunity does present itself,* and the voice on the other end of the phone—or the contact you've just met as a result of your networking—asks, "Could you send me your resume?" you don't want it to be several years out of date.

• **When you are ready to start looking for a job,** you may find it difficult to recall the details of the last several years of your career. The going will be easier and much more accurate if you update your resume as you go.

But don't limit your record keeping to a listing of company names and the dates of your employment. Whenever you achieve something significant—complete a project on time and under budget, prepare a marketing plan that is well received by your superiors and that ultimately succeeds in the market—make some brief notes about it. You may find it hard to believe at the moment that you could ever forget about such an accomplishment, but you might when you move on to the next one.

As you read the subsequent chapters, you'll find that these notes will also prove invaluable when you are preparing for an actual job interview.

Do consult a good book on resume writing when the time comes to put all this information into an appropriate format. One of the better ones is *The 90-Minute Resume* (see Appendix). It presents a technique for creating a good resume quickly by collaborating with a friend, spouse, or colleague.

Recommendation: Whatever guidebook you choose, be sure to select from the sample resumes shown the one that is most appropriate to your profession and your position within it. And have the finished product professionally printed; don't just run it off on the office copier.

Caution: Many resume services now prepare professional-looking resumes quickly using desktop publishing software and laser printers. This is fine, but steer clear of newsletterlike graphics such as pointing fingers, little stars, etc., unless you're in a creative field where you know that such touches will attract positive attention. With rare exception, your aim is to achieve a straightforward, classic look that conveys information without distracting from it.

Samples
Keep copies of business plans you have prepared, brochures you have designed, charts and graphs you have developed, articles you have written for industry publications—anything tangible that shows what you can do. These samples, too, can help you revise your resume and prepare a presentation for an interview. File them using whatever system is appropriate for you—by date, or by topic, or alphabetically—but not randomly. When you need some documentation, you want to be able to put your hands on it quickly, not have to go rummaging through cartons or desk drawers.

Personalized calling cards
In addition to your company business card, you might consider having a set of calling cards printed up with your name, home address, and phone number. Such cards can enhance your image, especially when you meet potentially valuable business contacts in a social setting. Also, if you would prefer that an individual call you at your home rather than at your office, it's much more polished to present your personal card, rather than to scratch out and write over the information on a company business card.

Observation: Many European businesspeople carry personalized calling cards, and you would thus make a strong positive impression on such a contact if you proffered a personalized card of your own.

The National Association for Female Executives, New

York City, suggests that your personal cards also be "career cards"—that they mention your profession or area of specialization. That can be especially helpful if you are considering a career change or would like your next position to have a slightly different focus from your present one.

If you do have personalized calling cards printed, don't cut corners on quality. Cheap print jobs look cheap, and will make you look as if you're trying to pass yourself off as something you're not. Get either engraved cards or ones with quality printing that closely resembles engraving. And do invest in high quality, heavyweight paper or card stock. Think, as corporations do, of the "return on investment"—the quality of the impression you'll make and the level for which you'll appear to be qualified, as compared with the cost.

Stay with classic colors, such as black type on a white or gray background, and a simple, easy-to-read typeface. And avoid the temptation to add additional sayings, graphics, or anything "cutesy" that could detract from your professional image.

Recommendation: Buy a brass or silver-toned case for your personalized cards and for your company business cards as well. They are available for less than ten dollars, and impress people to a degree that will astonish you.

Wardrobe

Wearing the appropriate clothing is an important part of creating the right impression in a job interview, and will be discussed in more detail in Chapter 4. However, buying a new outfit for each interview is hardly practical. So it's important that you always have one businesslike, conservative outfit that could take you to almost any interview on short notice.

Dinah Day, who is a consultant at the New York City executive outplacement firm Fuchs Cuthrell & Co., Inc., and is also an image director for private clients, suggests the following basics:

- *For men:* A gray pin-striped or navy suit, with a white pocket scarf; a tie with small polka dots or an understated design; and shoes that tie rather than slip on. Avoid flamboyant ties such as those by Hermes, she cautions: "People know how much they cost, and you don't want to look as though you're planning to take over the boss's office."
- *For women:* A navy suit or separates, with a white silk blouse, and either off-white or navy hose. Although pantsuits are acceptable at some companies, they are not appropriate for a job interview. Another caution: "Even in the fashion business, wait till you get the job before you wear a skirt that's above the knees."

Briefcase

Don't overlook the importance of this accessory in creating your professional image. Carry a briefcase—even if you're in an entry-level job—and you will look like an individual with a strong sense of personal worth, one who has his or her eye on the future.

Why do you need a briefcase if you aren't toting a sheaf of papers? Even if you're just carrying the daily newspaper, you don't want it in your hand, slipping about and falling into disarray, or leaving smudges on your clothing if you're wearing light colors. As for the quip about the person who has nothing to carry in a briefcase but a lunch bag—why not carry it there? It looks far better than clutching a brown bag. And you'll find that with a briefcase at your side, you feel better about your appearance and walk with greater self-assurance.

Moreover, when you go to a job interview, you don't want to be shuffling and juggling the forms you have to fill out, any samples you have brought with you, and the pad on which you are taking notes (see Chapter 5); it will simply be impossible for you to do all that and maintain your composure. You want everything organized—filed—in your briefcase, making you more comfortable and adding to the impression that you are a person who is in control.

Should a woman carry both a briefcase and a purse? Opinion is divided. But think about what's practical. When you open your briefcase, do you want any personal belongings to be visible? If you excuse yourself to go to the rest room, do you really want to carry your briefcase with you so that you can refresh your lipstick? If you don't want to be burdened with two things to carry, then keep your personal items in a small purse that fits neatly inside the briefcase and can be retrieved easily.

Appointment book

Massive, bulging appointment books that contain everything from your shopping list to the outline for your top project at work to the number of pounds you can bench press have become popular in recent years. If you feel that you must have such a book, either keep it at home or keep it out of sight at work. It is cumbersome and unprofessional looking—and, frankly, gives the impression that you don't attach any more importance to your lifetime goals than to your shopping list.

For use in a business setting, you want a small, good-quality book, preferably leather-bound; they .are not necessarily expensive. And keep it neat: No scraps of paper should tumble out when you turn the pages to see which week would be the most convenient for your lunch at the Drake with the marketing vice president of a Fortune 500 company.

Note: Do record personal appointments in this book, too, to avoid scheduling conflicts.

Answering machine

Most people nowadays have an answering machine at home. If you don't, because you rather like the idea of being able to hide somewhere, this is the time to change your views. If you're going to build a strong network, you want people to be able to reach you outside of office hours. And if you're unemployed, you will be away from home during the day, actively engaged in your job search, but must be able to receive messages just the same.

Caution: Your answering machine message should be brief and businesslike: "This is Jane Smith (or, You've reached 555–5757). Please leave your message after you hear the tone." Ask for the date and time to be included, if you wish, and stop there. Why tell the caller you can't come to the phone? Isn't that obvious? And this is not the occasion for impressing people with your comic ability. They will resent you wasting their time.

Activate your network

You know what you can and want to do. You know of some of the companies where you might be able to do those things. Your marketing tools are sharp. You're ready to start working on your job search.

When you actually *begin* the search, you'll be using three routes:

- Recruitment advertising placed by agencies or the potential employer
- Executive search firms
- Contacting companies directly

But you're not yet at the point of beginning your search. There's another step to be taken first: You need to activate your networks. Networking precedes your active job search, and should continue once you start to pursue the above three search routes. It's an essential tool that you never stop using, even after you land your desired job. But likely as not, it could use some sharpening.

The new networking

People have known for many years that they need to build a network of contacts if they want to be successful in their professional—and personal—lives. The idea isn't new, but the emphasis and the approach are.

"Network" has become a verb, as well as a noun. "You have to network," people say. It is something you *do*, as well as something you *build*. It is also something that many people do incorrectly. As a result, a body of rules and procedures has developed. There are even networking consultants.

Networking—and the contacts, information, and interviews that result—is such a significant part of the job search process, in fact, that it merits a chapter of its own. That chapter follows.

2

Get Set to Begin:
How to Make Your Net/work

"Networking is the most effective way to get a job."

You'll hear that again and again from your friends and colleagues, from outplacement counselors, career counselors, search firms. The reason so many people make the statement, of course, is that it is irrefutable: The more people you know, the more contacts you have, the better your chances of getting the kind of job you want when you want it.

The problem is, few people understand what the statement really means. Some people don't realize that they must take a "strategic, well-calculated approach" to networking, says Richard A. Hergenrather, president of the executive search firm Hergenrather & Co., in Hermosa Beach, California. There are those who are "very aggressive, and exploit a relationship. They don't recognize that there must be giving as well as taking."

Others make the mistake of leading with a request, he says. As soon as they find out what his profession is, they say something like, "Oh, my son is about to graduate from college. May I send you his resume?" Says Hergenrather, "Their approach is, 'I can *use* you.'" If the network is to work, "it's important to build a rapport, a relationship, so that people feel there's a fair exchange." Remember that networking is not collecting business cards; it is building relationships.

This is what networking doesn't mean: At a reception preceding a meeting of a group he has just joined, Joe Jobseeker walks up to a total stranger and says, "Hello, here's my business card. My name is Joe Jobseeker, and I'm looking for a job that's better than the one I have now." To which the stranger replies, "What luck, Joe! I'm Carl Contact, and you're just the kind of person I'd like to have working at the company of which I'm president. In fact, I'd like to groom you to be my successor. I hope you can start next Monday. Here's my card. Call me tomorrow and we'll meet for lunch to talk about the terms. I'm sure we'll be able to make you an offer that's attractive beyond your wildest dreams."

Ridiculous, right? Unfortunately, too many people expect that to happen and become impatient if it doesn't. They don't realize that networking is a long-term, multistep process that involves planning, focus, work—and very little "luck." As Nella G. Barkley, president of Crystal-Barkley Corporation, a career consulting and training firm headquartered in New York City, expresses it, "There's a prevalent attitude that if you join an organization, its members will fall down dead to advance your cause. It's simply not true."

People who hold that attitude are overlooking the underlying principle of networking, Barkley says. She explains that what networking *should* be is an exchange between people who share enthusiasms and mutual interests. "It is never taking advantage," she says.

To build a successful network, you must give before you can take. But in order to give to others, you must be visible and valuable. Thus the first step in building a network is not to look for contacts, but to make yourself visible to them. The difference is subtle, but significant.

How to make yourself visible

There are numerous ways to make yourself a high-profile person. This list is just a beginning. It should help you to think of other possibilities.

- *Join* industry associations, of course, but don't stop there. Hergenrather recommends breakfast clubs, informal groups of professionals in a specific field who hold regular information-sharing meetings. "Joining a breakfast club is a great way to stay on top of your industry and obtain job leads," he points out. Other possibilities he mentions are alumni associations or fund-raising or community redevelopment groups. Choose whatever is of genuine interest to you, and you will gain knowledge that you will enjoy and can share.
- *Volunteer* to work on committees within these groups, or to act as a mentor—whatever will enable you to use a skill you already have or develop one you would like to have. In the process, you'll also show yourself to be an active participant, not merely an observer.
- *Attend* trade conventions and management seminars, Hergenrather advises. At conventions you can rub shoulders with industry leaders, and learn about industry trends—and perhaps job openings—before they

become public knowledge. Management seminars, too, often bring you into contact with top people. But whether you meet such people or not, the knowledge you gain in the seminars will make you more valuable in your profession.

Observation: At industry meetings, you may very well find yourself side-by-side—while getting a drink, or at the lunch table—with someone whose office you would find it very difficult to get into. This is a key benefit of networking. Don't exploit it, like Joe Jobseeker, but do take advantage of it. Ask about the person's company—gather information—and offer information about yourself and your company. Use this opportunity to make conversation as you would with any peer—because in this setting, you are peers.

- *Write* articles for company publications or industry journals. Such articles build your reputation as an authority in your industry. If you don't yet have the competence to write such an article, or don't have an idea for one, start small. Write letters to the editors of such publications, responding to articles that they have printed. Explain why you either support or disagree with one or more of the ideas presented in the article, and point out what it is in your background that makes you an authority on the subject: "As a salesperson for a company that markets prescription drugs, some of which are controversial, I have often had to give the rationale behind . . ."

- *Speak* to industry or community groups. Look broadly at the possibilities. When Dr. Barbara A. Pletcher, a former college professor and founder of the National Association for Professional Saleswomen, began her career as a real estate broker, she offered to speak to community groups, gratis, on such subjects as management principles or communication. Her presentation contained no "commercials" for her business; she simply wanted to become known in her community, so that people would think of her when the time came to call a broker.

- *Teach* at a local community college.
- *Lead* a youth group.
- *Help out* at the PTA.
- *What else* can you think of?

Each of the bulleted activities above adds to your store of information, some of which you will eventually have the opportunity to share in a social or a business situation. You will also develop managerial and organizational skills, many of which are transferable to a work setting. And all of this gives you more to offer to everyone you meet.

Of course, some of the connections you make in these activities will develop into friendships. You'll get together on an informal basis with the people you've met simply because you like each other and want to know more about each other. And so your network will grow.

Observation: As you read the above list of suggestions, it should become clear that you are always doing a certain amount of personal and professional networking: developing contacts who at some point will provide information or assistance that you need, or refer you to someone else who can. The difference now is that you need to develop a more *organized* approach to networking, and *focus on the objective* of getting a job.

Job Hunting While Working

Networking is the key to looking for a job while you are employed. Not only do many networking activities take place outside of the workday, but those that are scheduled during regular working hours are pursuits that your management will actually encourage. You're doubtful? Take another look at the list.

How to build your network

Your ongoing research, as described in Chapter 1, should have uncovered companies that interest you. Joan Learn, of the Greenwich Group, advises people to compile a list of twenty or twenty-five companies that they would like to work for. There will come a time when you can ask the people in your network for names of people in those companies.

When that time comes, "You don't say, 'Do you know of anyone who has a job for me?'" Learn cautions. "You simply ask, 'Do you know anybody in any of these companies?' You want to get names," she says. "This approach takes time, and is not natural for some people. But they can become comfortable with it."

Observation: If it is uncomfortable for you or seems artificial, just think of how easily it works in your private life: "Do you know the name of the maître d' at any of these restaurants?" "Do you know a hairdresser at any of these salons?" "Do you know which hardware stores might carry these brands of hand tools?" "Do you know anyone who . . . ?" It's a simple request for information; you're not asking for any kind of recommendation or commitment.

Once you have a name, you have a specific person to call. Even if it's the wrong person for your purpose, if you are able to explain succinctly what your purpose is (we'll get to that below), he or she can—and usually will—direct you to the right one.

As you are building your network of new names, don't overlook the names you already have. Duke Foster, Jr., senior vice president in the Stamford, Connecticut, office of Korn/Ferry International, the world's largest executive search firm, emphasizes that you should "consider all sources—people from your childhood, high school, college, military service, jobs, neighbors, friends, peers, subordinates, superiors, the Little League. List everyone you believe would help you if they could—if it wouldn't cost them anything. Make recruiters part of your network, too," he urges. How? By sending them your resume (see Chapter 3).

Keep a network diary

Obviously, your network is going to grow dramatically. The only way to keep track of it, and to use it properly, is with a network diary. Use a large-format book that is loose-leaf, so that you can rearrange the pages as necessary, and keep the names in order—either alphabetically, or grouped by appropriate subjects.

Allow one page per person, although some people will eventually require more. On that page, record when and where you met the person, the circumstances of your meeting—for example, who introduced you—and why you want to keep in touch with the person. Keep a record of phone calls and face-to-face meetings, with dates, brief summaries of what happened, who promised to do what when, and what your next move should be.

It helps to include personal as well as business-related facts that come up in the conversation. For example, "His son Doug is a finalist in the national high school history club competition." A quick look at your notes before the next phone call or get-together will give you the small talk you need—"How did Doug make out with his history project?" It will also make a strongly favorable impression on the other person, whose reaction will be something like, "Imagine his remembering Doug's project."

A sample diary page

Name and title Allen Lewis/Regional sales manager
Company name Brewster Chemicals
Address 3231 Saxon Rd., Brewster, PA
Telephone number 215-555-0000
Fax number 215-555-1001
Place and date met Linda Campbell's concert—2/13
How met Linda introduced us (they attend the same church)
Discussed what A public speaking course he just started attending; he finds it very helpful in his work
Reason to follow up I could use some help with speaking in public
Follow-up promised (action, date) Allen said he'd let me know when the March meeting is, so I can attend if I'm interested
Call him if haven't heard by 2/27

Action taken Allen did call—2/22—with information about 3/11 meeting

Met again At 3/11 speakers' group meeting

Discussed what (And so on, for the rest of the page—and as many more as are necessary.)

Note: At the speakers' meeting, you will not only acquire some public speaking skills—the first benefit you will realize—but will also begin to meet people whose names will eventually be added to your networking diary. Thus the network grows.

Observation: This diary is not as big an undertaking as it seems. You already record this kind of information on bits and scraps of paper, don't you? All you're doing now is keeping it together in one place.

Requesting a networking interview

It's now time to get in touch with some of the other people whose names you have been collecting—the ones your contacts have told you about. It's usually preferable to begin with a letter, both to avoid "telephone tag" and to increase your chances of getting past the "gatekeeper," the secretary. In the letter, tell the recipient when you will call to set up an appointment—and do so. Then, when you make that call, you can legitimately tell the secretary that you are following up on a letter you sent and that Mr. Throckmorton is expecting your call.

The most effective way to get your letter read is to open with the name of your mutual acquaintance (always making sure to get the individual's permission before doing so): "Dear Mr. Throckmorton: Wilbur Smedley suggested that I write to you." Throckmorton will surely read on to find out why his old buddy Smedley would have given you his name.

You may or may not have told Smedley your reasons for wanting to arrange a meeting. But that doesn't matter. You simply wanted to identify Throckmorton, and now you want him to continue past the first sentence of your letter. So it's up to you to explain, specifically and persuasively, what you want and how much of his time it will take.

It's wise to ask for only fifteen to thirty minutes of the person's time. Anything more is truly taking advantage. What you ask for depends on your specific circumstances.

Example: "I have an idea for thus-and-such and would appreciate your opinion of its potential."

Example: "I'm in a career transition and would like to ask you about the opportunities in this field."

Example: "I read thus-and-such about your company and would like to get some information about it."

Example: "I'd like to get your feelings about trends in your industry. I have some ideas and I'd like to share them."

Example: "Your company's way of handling thus-and-such has always interested me. I'd like to ask you some questions about it."

Observation: If you have already met the person at an industry gathering, you're one step ahead. You can open with, "I enjoyed talking with you at the Foodservice Distributors meeting on Tuesday. Your comments on reducing losses intrigued me, and . . ." Then segue into one of the examples above.

The cardinal rules. Conspicuously absent from the preceding list of examples is any mention of a job with the individual's company. And it must *not* be mentioned.

As Learn of the Greenwich Group points out, "The cardinal rules of networking are 'Never ask for a job; ask for suggestions' and 'Never ask for favors; ask for advice.'"

At this point you may be wondering, Won't it be hard to think up something to ask the individual about? On the contrary: You shouldn't have to "think up" anything. If you have been researching fields that genuinely interest you, and companies within those fields, numerous subjects will present themselves. But if you are not aware of a reason for requesting a meeting with an individual, you should not do so. If you meet to discuss a subject that you have had to force yourself to "think up," the encounter will be both awkward and unproductive.

You may also wonder why anyone would actually agree to meet with you just for the purpose of providing you with information. The reason is that it boosts a person's ego to be sought out as an authority on a subject, or as a role model, or to be told that he or she is in a position to help you. Thus you may find that quite a few people are willing to give of themselves as long as you are serious about what you are doing.

Observation: Willing and eager though people may be, they are also very busy—in meetings, out of town, or whatever. If you don't get through the first time you telephone, don't be surprised or discouraged; be persistent. Ask the assistant when the person will be available, and what would be the best time to call. Find out the assistant's name, too—"Are you her assistant? May I have your name, please?"—and use it when you call back. You may find that that one courtesy gains you an ally, and gets your phone call through.

Note: Using the word "assistant" rather than "secretary" may earn you points, too.

The networking interview

This is the moment of truth, the culmination of your networking efforts. You are face-to-face with a person who truly could be of significant help to you. Moreover, you aren't being *interviewed*—although you will, of course, be presenting information about yourself in the course of the conversation. Unlike in a job interview, *you* are the person in control; *you* set the agenda.

How can you make the most of the encounter? By following these suggestions:

- **Be prepared.** Arrive armed with a list of specific questions that you would like to have answered.
- **Be informed.** Show that you've already given the subject some thought, and want to do more than just pick the person's brain. If you truly have researched the field, and can offer information as well as requesting it, you are giving as well as taking. And that makes you more valuable to your contact.
- **Take notes.** If you don't, you give the distinct impression that the information isn't important to you and isn't your real reason for requesting the meeting.
- **Adhere to your time limit.** About five minutes before the end of the limit that you have specified, say something like "Our time is nearly up—I don't want to take advantage of your generosity. There's just one more point I'd like to ask you about." If your contact wants to continue the conversation, he or she will say so. But it's up to you to indicate your integrity by keeping to your original agreement.
- **Expand the network.** Just before leaving, ask the

contact if he or she can suggest anyone else with whom you could discuss this subject. If you've handled yourself professionally, and have shown genuine interest in the subject and the contact, he or she probably will provide another name. It's yet another opportunity to demonstrate to you that he or she is authoritative and well connected. Thus you're much more likely to be told "Yes, I think you might also want to talk with Helen Highpower—she's a good friend of mine," rather than "Sorry, I really don't know anybody else who's familiar with this."

- *Be appreciative.* Thank Throckmorton on the spot for his time and his willingness to share such important information with you. And follow up with a note reinforcing that statement. The note should be "precise and timely," Barkley stresses. "Don't write a letter that could be written to anybody; it won't remain in someone's file." Instead, include a specific reference to a subject that was discussed or a point that was made. Focus on the other person: "You were especially kind on such a busy day" vs. "I was so glad to have an opportunity to meet with you. . . ."

Barkley also suggests using the note to "position yourself for a return." For example, you might promise to get back to the person when you find the answer to a question that arose during the interview, or to let him or her know the outcome of a suggestion that was made. And send that note within a week to ten days, she urges.

- *Resist temptation.* What if, at some point during the meeting, your contact says the words you may have been secretly hoping for: "I think we could use someone like you"? *The worst thing you can do,* says Barkley, is to say hopefully, "'Oh, thank you. . . .'

The information freezes and dries up," she says, "and you're sent down the hall to fill out an employment application."

Barkley says emphatically, "You can't make a liar out of yourself by contradicting your reason for requesting the meeting. If you want to change your reason, you do so *after* the meeting." The proper way to handle the situation, she says, is with a response like "I'm pleased to know that you think of me in this regard. What is your timetable? I'd like to give this some thought and get back to you within that time." To make this work, Barkley says, "You have to *believe* that information is necessary to make a good decision, and you must value yourself enough to gather that information."

Observation: Why go through all this effort if it's not to get a job? You do it in order to gain information that makes you a more valuable person in your current job—and a stronger contender when you do begin to look for a new job. You also do it to add this individual to your network. It's a never-ending process.

Record of networking meetings

Your network diary is a record of everyone you meet, however casually, whom you want to keep as part of your network. But the meetings that you *request* are focused, and should have both an objective and an outcome. To maintain your focus and track your results, make up a form with the following headings:

- Name and title
- Company name
- Address

- Telephone number
- Fax number
- Assistant's name
- Contact and connection (the person who gave you this name, and how they know each other)
- Reason for requesting a meeting
- Date of letter requesting meeting
- Date(s) of follow-up phone call(s)
- Date of interview
- Questions to be asked
- Outcome of meeting (you may simply want to attach your notes)
- Thank-you letter sent
- Follow-up action taken

Don't stop with one follow-up. Take more actions. Keep your network alive.

How to short-circuit the network

If you lose your focus, fail to observe the proper etiquette, or fail to follow up, you'll lose the value of your networking meetings. Here are two examples:

A neophyte's wrong turns. When Ellen Johnson, an editor at a business magazine, answered her telephone, the voice on the other end said, "Hello, Miss Johnson, my name is Nick Ransom. I just graduated from state university with a degree in literature. I read about you in the alumni magazine and wondered if I could come in and talk to you. I'm interested in getting into publishing, and thought maybe you could give me some ideas."

Without a moment's hesitation, Ellen said yes, and scheduled an appointment on the day that Nick would be in town. She was impressed with Nick's initiative and courage in calling a total stranger, and was eager to help a fellow alumnus. She was also flattered to know that *someone* had read about her in the column on successful alumni and thought of her as an authority in her field.

The interview began badly. On the appointed day, at the appointed time, Ellen was engrossed in her work when she heard a small voice say, "Hi—I'm Nick." She was surprised to see him standing in her doorway—she had expected the receptionist to let her know when he arrived. But Nick had managed to bypass the receptionist and just wander about until he found Ellen's office. All right, she thought, maybe someone who just graduated wouldn't know that you were supposed to see the receptionist and be announced. But what about the scruffy clothing? Wrinkled shirt and trousers, zip-front jacket. This wasn't a job interview, of course, but it was a business meeting.

It went downhill from there. For the next twenty minutes Ellen tried to tell Nick how he should go about looking for a job in the publishing field, what duties were required in entry-level jobs, and what the salary range would probably be. Although Nick did ask an occasional question, they were usually on the order of "You work that many hours a day?" or "They really give you only two weeks of vacation?" And he made it quite clear that he didn't think much of the superficial requirements of the business world—regimented clothing, for example.

Initially enthusiastic, Ellen eventually sensed the futility of it all. Clearly, Nick had hoped their connection would mean that she would offer him a job. When the meeting finally ended, she said to him in exasperation, "I know you're not going to agree with this, but you really should wear a suit when you go for a job interview. It does make a difference."

Nick had certainly started out correctly when he phoned. He immediately established the connection, and told Ellen exactly what he wanted. But from then on, he totally missed the point. Had he been receptive to what she told him during their meeting, she might have suggested they keep in touch, even acted as his mentor. And there might very well have come a time when there would have been a job available for him within her organization, or when she could have passed his name on to a colleague who needed to hire someone. But because Nick totally misunderstood what networking is all about, he missed out on what could have been a major opportunity for him.

A pro slips up. After several years as a saleswoman for a major insurance company, Barbara Sullivan wanted to make a career change. The hotel industry appealed to her because of the possibility of travel, and she hoped her sales experience would be directly transferable.

To find out more about opportunities in the industry and how relevant her own background was, Barbara worked at meeting the various hotel industry members of an organization for sales professionals to which she belonged. Through them she eventually obtained the name of the top sales executive in the nearby regional sales office of a leading hotel chain, and was able to schedule a networking interview with him.

Barbara's interview with Eric Allen was even more encouraging than she'd hoped it would be. He was eager to meet her because the person who had given her his name was a close friend. Barbara had done her homework. She could see that Eric was impressed with her knowledge of his company.

And he seemed pleased, rather than annoyed, when she explained that she would be talking with people at other hotel chains. She wanted to learn about the differences in their offerings, their target markets, and their objectives, in order to get a feeling for where she would fit in best. "I like your thoroughness" was the way he put it. But he suggested that she also talk with other people in his own company, and said he would check to see who else might be available to meet with her.

At the end of the interview, Eric shook Barbara's hand warmly and said, "I hope your search works out well for you."

Barbara was sure something good would come out of this interview. Talking with Eric only reinforced the strong positive feelings she'd already formed about his company. So she couldn't understand why days, then weeks, passed and she never heard another word. He had said he'd get other names for her. Had he been unable to do so? Had he forgotten about her? What could possibly have gone wrong?

All of Barbara's careful research and preparation came to naught because of her own errors. She never showed her appreciation by sending a follow-up note thanking Eric for his time and the information he'd provided. In that note, she should, of course, have also reiterated her understanding of who was to call whom, so that she could get the names of additional contacts. But she'd already erred on this point by not clarifying it, and writing it down, during the interview. Afterward, she simply couldn't remember who was supposed to do the calling and was embarrassed to call Eric, in case it was he who was supposed to call her.

Because Barbara never followed up in any way, Eric assumed that she was no longer interested in his company, was annoyed that she never let him know that, and felt that the time he'd spent with her was completely wasted. He shared these feelings with his close friend, the original networking contact. As a result, he, too, cut Barbara from his network.

Job Hunting While Working

A sudden change in your behavior—long lunch hours, coming to work dressed much better than usual—can alert your manager to the fact that you are looking for a job. But if you are regularly involved in networking activities that require the occasional long lunch or dressier outfit, such things are less likely to attract attention. Which means that you may in fact be able to schedule a lunchtime interview without anyone noticing anything out of the ordinary.

What if you need to carry along large samples of your work that you normally keep at the office? Put them in the trunk of your car the night before. Or, suggests an engineer who uses public transportation, "Pay the guy at the candy stand in the lobby a couple of bucks to hold them for you."

Keep your network alive

Frequent communication with the people in your network is a must. Let them know how you're doing, and how they're helping. Get in touch with Smedley. If he is a personal friend of yours, a phone call may be all that's necessary: "Thanks for referring me to Throckmorton—I got great information from him on global strategies."

Following up is also important to keep yourself alive in your contact's mind, says Foster. But keep it positive, he emphasizes. "Call and tell the person something it would be helpful for him to know. For example, 'I read a fascinating article about the executive search business the other day that said . . . Would you like me to send you a copy?' That's marketing," Foster says, "but people don't do it."

Although networking may eventually lead to a job, you shouldn't rely on this technique exclusively. As you can see, it can be a very slow process. Thus, if you are seriously in the market for a new job, you must also be trying to schedule interviews that are job-specific. Techniques for lining up such interviews are discussed in the next chapter.

3

Begin:
How to Get Interviews

As crucial as it is to develop your network, as helpful as the network can be, you cannot rely on it exclusively when you are actively looking for a job. You must also consider the three other routes that were mentioned in Chapter 1:

- Recruitment advertising placed by agencies or the potential employer
- Executive search firms
- Contacting companies directly

Recruitment advertising

Dozens—sometimes hundreds—of people respond to a single employment ad. How can you even be noticed, let alone called in for an interview? The key is to tailor your response to the specific ad. A generic "In response to your ad, I am enclosing a resume" just doesn't cut it.

American Airlines, Inc., places ads for professional positions in *The Wall Street Journal*, local newspapers, and professional and technical publications. It's important for respondents to "create linkage between what they have and what I need," says Michael Riley, manager of recruitment and personnel services for the Dallas, Texas, company. "They must show on paper that they have what I requested in the ad."

Write a targeted cover letter in which you call attention to a specific section of your resume, or give greater detail about something mentioned only briefly in the resume, or both.

Example: Your ad in Sunday's *Newspaper* requested responses from individuals who have had experience managing promotional campaigns for consumer products. Please note on the enclosed resume that during my years with Bearns & Lewis I was responsible for the Super Bowl promotion for Krunchy-Munchies. That responsibility included determining the media schedule and . . .

Nothing is too obvious or too insignificant to mention in your cover letter if it is stated in the ad. "Our ad specifically says that there will be a lot of telephone work," one manager lamented, "and not one of these letters of application says anything about having telephone experience."

You may also want to prepare more than one resume if your skills and experience are such that your career could go in more than one direction. In that case, enclose whichever resume is relevant for a prospective employer.

Recommendation: If you are responding to an ad

placed by an employment agency, and your initial contact is either by telephone or in person, be equally targeted in what you say. Help the counselor at the agency to see what it is that makes you uniquely qualified for the position. He or she can then present that information to the prospective employer, again increasing the chances that the employer will want to meet with you.

Should you answer blind ads? An old—very old—joke tells of the person who inadvertently answered a blind ad for his own job. Practically speaking, the chances of that happening are very slim. How likely is it that your company, unbeknownst to you, would be planning to fill your job at the same time that you, unbeknownst to them, would be looking for a change? And that you would be unable to recognize a description of your own job?

But if the unlikely does occur, and your manager rattles your resume under your nose and demands, "What's the meaning of this?" your response should be the same as if any other aspect of your secret search were discovered, says Loretta Berardi, a partner in the executive search firm DeSilva & Stentiford Associates, Ltd., New York City. The response she suggests: "I feel that my career has been blocked here. I don't see any opportunity to move on, so I'm exploring my options."

Read the employment advertising for positions throughout your industry, not just at your level. Reading those ads can give you an indication of which companies are hiring, what kinds of positions they are filling, and what the salary ranges are for positions above and below yours (thus giving you some clue as to what they would be at your level).

Executive search firms

Many jobs at upper levels are never advertised. Instead, companies hire search firms—often referred to as "headhunters"—to seek qualified candidates for those positions. "When we do a search," Berardi explains, "several of us work on it. We assess people and assess the market very thoroughly. The principals in our firm read all the trade publications for their areas of specialization, and get to know people. Anyone who gets press is noticed. And we call our contacts."

Thus search firms may very well hear about you if you've been busy making yourself visible, building a reputation in your profession, and expanding your network. But you don't need to sit back and wait for that to happen. You can, and should, *send your resume to search firms*.

Observation: You may have heard or read otherwise. There is a great deal of confusion about what search firms are and what they do.

There are two kinds of executive search firms: retained and contingency. The difference between the two is said to be of greater importance to the employer than to the candidate. But if you are going to approach firms on your own, you should be aware of the distinction.

- *Retained search firms* are hired—"retained"—to conduct a search to fill a specific position. They are compensated whether or not they find someone to fill the position. They may specialize in certain fields, and usually fill jobs paying salaries of sixty thousand dollars and up. Their mission is to find qualified candidates for the employer, and they frequently approach individuals who are not actively looking for jobs. (In the past, some retained firms would consider only people who were employed. But these days, being unemployed carries no stigma and is in no way an indication of less-than-top quality.) Because finding a job for a candidate is not the major concern of these firms, there are those who say it is a waste of time to send your resume to them. Not so.

- *Contingency search firms* may conduct a search at a company's request, but also will work to place an individual who is seeking a new job. Thus they may be more approachable than retained firms. They are compensated only if they place someone, and generally handle jobs in the forty to sixty thousand dollar range.

- *Adding to the confusion,* you may find both types of search firms, as well as employment agencies and consultants, listed in telephone directories under a heading such as "Personnel Consulting Firms," "Personnel Placement Firms," "Personnel Recruiting Firms," or "Personnel Services."

An efficient way to identify search firms you wish to contact—or to check on any that may contact you—is to look in one of the industry directories. They are available in public and university libraries, but the prices are reasonable enough that you may wish to purchase your own copies from the publishers (see Appendix). *The Directory of Executive Recruiters* identifies search firms as either retained or contingency and gives their fields of specialization, the minimum salaries for the positions they handle, and the key contact at the firm. *The National Directory of Personnel Consultants* lists mainly contingency firms, plus some retained firms, and gives the address and contact name for each.

How to approach search firms

Once you have identified the search firms that are appropriate for your field and your salary range, you can send your resume, with a cover letter, to the contact listed in the directory.

It's preferable to make your initial contact with a recruiter when you are not urgently seeking a position, advises Foster of Korn/Ferry. Your cover letter should clarify your status. He suggests two possible formats for that statement.

Example: "I'm not in the job market at the moment, but would like you to keep my resume on file."

Example: "I've done a great job at ABC Co., but I think that someday I might be interested in doing thus-and-such."

When you are ready to look in earnest, he says, you can write to any search firms you have previously contacted, telling the recruiters of your change in status.

Example: "I promised to let you know when I was ready to do some serious looking—and the time is now."

But if your initial contact is made when you are already doing the serious looking, say so. And be specific about your reason for leaving, Foster urges.

Example: "I'm leaving my company because the Dubuque office is being closed (or—because my job is being eliminated) and am therefore sending you my resume."

Your cover letter should state whether or not you are willing to relocate and, if so, which areas are acceptable to you. "It's also a good idea," Foster says, "to indicate the future career directions that are attractive to you. And if you want to make a career change, explain why." The more you can tell the executive recruiter about yourself, the better his or her chances of making a good match between you and a prospective employer.

If the search firm to which you're writing has more than one office, write to all the locations that you are interested in, Foster urges. You cannot rely on a data processing or other clerical person to route you through the entire system. And he issues two warnings for individuals who choose to work through executive search firms:

- *Don't* contact the search firm retained by your employer if you are still employed and have not told your company that you plan to leave. The search firm will simply discard your resume.
- *Do* phone if you say in your letter that you will do so. "It's astounding how many people say they'll call and then don't," Foster remarks. "Because I'm expecting the call, I put the resume next to the phone so I'll be prepared to speak to the person. When weeks go by, and I don't hear anything, I assume the person got a job. So I toss the resume—and it never even gets into our computer."

Follow up in any case, whether or not you have said you will. Berardi suggests checking back about every six weeks, preferably in writing. Remind the recruiters that you are still interested and available, and mention any change in your status. Don't badger them, however. Remember that retained search firms, in particular, work for companies, not individuals, and won't go looking for a job for you.

And if, for any reason, you no longer want to be considered, let recruiters know. This is not a relationship you can afford to mishandle. You never know when a recruiter may come across your name in the course of doing a search; you want the recollection to be positive.

When a search firm contacts you

Getting a phone call from an executive recruiter is exciting and flattering. Maybe this will be the big break you've been waiting for. Be cautious, however; there's a lot you need to find out before you proceed:

- *Ask questions about the recruiter.* Because no licensing requirements exist, there are no restrictions on the use of the term "executive recruiter." Thus you should try to determine the recruiter's legitimacy and credibility. Ask if the recruiter is operating on a retained or contingency basis, if this is an exclusive assignment, where the office is located, and what the professional affiliations are. Because you should not make any commitment at this point, you can check the recruiter's credentials in one of the directories mentioned above before your next conversation.
- *Ask questions about the job.* Even if the recruiter does not want to name the hiring company yet, you should be able to find out the approximate location and size, the position's title and salary range, and why the recruiter is considering you as a candidate.
- *Ask about the next step.* You need time to check the recruiter's credentials and think about whether or not you're interested. How soon does the recruiter want to hear from you? Many recruiters will want to meet with

you to tell you more about the position and perhaps do a preliminary screening. Recruiter Berardi says that after a member of her firm has told a candidate about the position and the company, "We have them send us a follow-up letter explaining why they think they're suitable for the position, and we use that letter to screen them."

- *Proceed only if you're genuinely interested.* Don't go through the process simply because you're flattered or curious. If a recruiter senses that you're a perennial job applicant and are wasting his or her time, you won't be considered for future positions.

The direct approach

As you've been networking, you've developed a list of companies in which you are interested. You've approached some of those companies through your contacts in the network. But now it's time to get in touch with the others on your own.

Caution: If a search firm is trying to match you up with a particular company, never circumvent the search firm and contact the company directly. You'll knock yourself right out of the running.

This time, when you contact a company, your objective is not merely to get information, but to get an interview with the person who has the authority to hire you.

Zero in on the right person. When you answer an ad, or a search firm matches you up with a potential employer, you may very well have your first interview—a screening interview—with a human resources person. That person will then move you along to the appropriate hiring manager. If this is the accepted procedure, any resistance on your part will immediately eliminate you from the competition. (More about that in Chapter 5.)

But when you make the first move, it's different. It's appropriate—and necessary—for you to try to bypass human resources, which might try to screen you out if there is no immediate need for your services. You want to try to get directly to a hiring manager who could spot your potential.

It is sometimes suggested that applicants identify the appropriate person by looking in the company's annual report or in various business directories. But all of those sources have one or more shortcomings: They may list only three or four of the top executives, and may not include the level—or the functional area—in which you are interested. They may represent first names by initials only; it's hard to sell yourself persuasively when your letter opens with "Dear P. Smith." And, of course, changes in personnel and titles occur.

The most effective way to get the name you need is to call the company directly. Simply say, honestly, that you want to write to a particular individual. No one will ever ask you what you are planning to write. And you will be able to obtain an enormous amount of information.

Example: "Good morning, Acme Company."

"Good morning. I'd like to write to the person who handles your company's sales training programs. Can you tell me who that is?"

"That would be either Mr. Lawson or Mr. Bennett."

"Thank you. Can you connect me to Mr. Bennett's assistant so I can find out if he's the right person. [You can get through to anyone's assistant.] And would you please give me the direct number in case we get disconnected."

"Of course—the number is 555–2645."

* * *

"Good morning—Mr. Bennett's office, Sharon Winters speaking."

"Good morning, Miss Winters. I'm trying to find out who is responsible for Acme's sales training programs so I can send him a letter. I believe it's either Mr. Lawson or Mr. Bennett, but I'm not sure which." [Notice how well-informed and authoritative you already sound.]

"Actually, they're both involved. Mr. Lawson is the training director, but he reports to Mr. Bennett."

"Thank you, that helps a lot. I think Mr. Bennett is the person I should write to. Could you please tell me his full name and title?"

"Of course. It's James T.—as in Thomas—Bennett—double n, double t. His title is director of sales and marketing."

Neither the receptionist nor Miss Winters gave out any information they should not have given out. But you have learned, in just a few minutes, what the reporting relationships are, the full name and title of the person to whom you want to address your letter, and his direct phone number—so that you can get through more quickly when you make your follow-up phone call.

Observation: The rule of thumb is that you should approach the person who is two levels above the level at which you hope to be hired. That is the person who has the authority to hire you. "Never write to a peer," says Foster. "If you're a vice president of finance, and you write to a company's vice president of finance to say you're looking for a job, you are in effect saying that you're looking for his job."

Start with a letter. This is the time to come right out and say you are looking for a job. Any subterfuge or pretense will only work against you. Enclose your resume. Explain in your cover letter exactly what skills and experience you have to offer and what kind of job you are interested in, and specifically ask for an interview.

"If you send an unsolicited resume, remember that you are one of many, so get to the point fast in your cover letter," says Riley at American Airlines. "Don't write a lengthy introduction. Say something like 'I have an MBA in finance in this area and am looking for this kind of job.' People tend to go on and on."

Riley says that he will circulate an unsolicited resume to appropriate managers, and it helps everyone if the applicant says what he or she wants to do. If you are interested in two different kinds of jobs, he adds, write twice, using a different, targeted cover letter each time.

Follow up with a phone call. End your letter by saying that you will call at a specified time—usually about two weeks after the person will receive the letter. Call when you say you will, and tell the assistant—in truth—that you are following up on your letter to Mr. Bennett and that he is expecting your call.

If he's unavailable, which is likely, ask the assistant what the best time is to reach him—again, information that is relatively easy to obtain. (Remember to address the assistant by name if you know it.) And keep calling. If an interview with this person is important to you—and you shouldn't have even started the process if it isn't— you can't let yourself be deterred by the difficulty of getting through to a busy individual.

Chances are good that you will eventually get through. It's unlikely that Mr. Bennett will ask Miss Winters to "tell that nuisance Norwood to stop calling!" And when you do get through to Bennett, make your pitch. Repeat what you have to offer, and ask if you can come in to talk with him for fifteen minutes or half an hour about the possibilities for you at his company.

Will you get an appointment? To begin with, your initiative and nerve will be impressive. Secondly, if you have chosen the company using the right criteria, you do have something to offer. It will be in Bennett's interest to spend a few minutes learning about you, whether there's an immediate opening for you or not. Companies do conduct interviews when they're not hiring, so that they'll have a pool of qualified candidates ready if they need to move fast. Thus, if Mr. Bennett does say that there are no openings for you at this time, try this: "I can appreciate that. But would you be willing to talk with me just so you'll know more about my qualifications when something does open up?"

We've been cautioning you against indulging in fantasies about jobs that somehow materialize. This is not one of those fantasies. People do, in real life, make cold calls like this and get hired for positions that are about to be available and are about to be advertised.

Recommendation: Your chances of success will be greater if you have some small and medium-sized companies on your list, especially in tougher times. Many people want to work at high-profile companies, so there's more competition for the jobs such firms have to offer. Also, smaller or newer companies are more likely to be expanding, so there may be more job opportunities there than you'd expect.

If you diligently pursue all three avenues—employment advertising, search firms, and direct contact—all the while keeping your network active, you will unquestionably, even unavoidably, get interviews. This is not your ultimate objective, however. You want to succeed in the interviews.

It was Woody Allen, we believe, who quipped that "90 percent of success in life is just showing up." Unfortunately, that's not true when it comes to interviewing. You need to do far more than show up at the appointed time. In order to succeed, you must prepare in great detail for that appearance. Chapter 4 will show you what and how to prepare.

Job Hunting While Working

Scheduling a job interview while you are still employed is not as difficult as you might think. Prospective employers do not seriously expect you to walk off the job at 10:30 A.M. to meet with them. Appointments can be scheduled during the lunch hour, after hours, or even on weekends for jobs at some levels. If none of those is a possibility, take a personal day.

But don't fake a dentist appointment or your grandmother's funeral. You don't want to be in the position of giving such an explanation when a prospective employer asks you how you were able to get time off for the interview: "Where does your boss think you are now?" The answer reveals the way you treat your present manager—and will probably treat the next one.

Job Hunting While Working

If you are concerned about getting telephone calls at work from prospective employers or search firms you have contacted, consider giving such people the telephone number for your home answering machine. Indicate that on your resume by putting the word (message), in parentheses, after your phone number. You might state in your answering machine message that you will return calls on the next business day. Or, if you can, program the answering machine so that you can pick up the messages from another telephone and perhaps return the calls that same day.

4

How to Prepare
for Job Interviews

Showing up is not enough for job-interview success. Even showing up on time is not enough (although not doing so will cost you dearly). But being good at what you do isn't good enough, either: There are too many other people who are just as well qualified for a particular position as you are.

The only way to distinguish yourself from the competition is to present your qualifications and yourself more effectively and persuasively than others do. To achieve that, you must prepare thoroughly by taking the following steps in order:

- Research the company at which you will be interviewed
- Identify your key strengths and achievements
- Review your personal history
- Plan your presentation
- Anticipate the questions

- Rehearse, rehearse, rehearse
- Prepare mentally
- Prepare physically

Research the company

Yes, you have been researching industries and companies in the earlier stages of your job search, as you were "getting ready" and "starting" and "beginning." But this is different. When you have an appointment for a job interview, for the specific purpose of determining whether or not you should be added to a company's staff, you need to learn everything you possibly can about that company. The depth of your knowledge will help persuade the interviewer or interviewers that you are genuinely interested in working for the company.

Thus you should certainly try to find out the company's major products or services, who its customers and competitors are, its annual sales or revenues, its financial history, and the names of its officers and directors.

Start your research on a company by reading its annual report. If the timing is such that the annual report is somewhat out of date—the new one is about to be published—ask for quarterly updates. Also ask for 10K financial statements. If the company is privately held, ask for a company history or backgrounder. Newsletters aimed at employees and customers can help, too.

If you are working with a search firm, you may be able to get some of the information and literature you need from the recruiter. Otherwise, call the company directly.

Recommendation: If you don't already have a contact at the company who can provide these materials for you, phone the company and ask for public relations, or communications, or investor relations. Eventually you'll reach someone who can tell you who the proper person is.

Next check directories and magazine articles. The former are a quick source of information on annual sales, product lines, and names of key officials. You'll find them at public or university libraries. The latter will help you fill in the bigger picture—the company's competitors, its market position, and its strategy. It also helps to read articles written by the company's president or CEO, or ones in which those officials are quoted, for insight into its operating style and goals.

Check one or more of the following sources for basic facts about corporations. You will need this information for the "Company Profile Sheet" we'll suggest that you put together for each firm that grants you an interview (see page 63). Note that while there is some duplication among these sources, you may have to consult more than one to complete your research.

- *Directory of Corporate Affiliations.* Lists the divisions, subsidiaries, and affiliates of every major U.S. corporation. Useful for seeing relationships and also for identifying the parent companies of entities that do not have their own listings in other directories.
- *Everybody's Business.* For 400 top companies, gives market rankings of specific products and services plus comments on workplace conditions and corporate social responsibility.
- *Encyclopedia of Business Information Sources.* The source of sources; lists directories, books, organizations, periodicals, and other sources of information on subjects of interest to managerial personnel.

- *Million Dollar Directory.* Lists the 50,000 top public and private U.S. companies; gives sales volume, number of employees, industry classifications, officers and directors, and bank, accounting, and legal firm relationships.
- *Moody's Manuals.* Two volumes of financial and business information—including company history—for 5,000 major corporations and institutions in one hundred countries; plus additional volumes on the transportation, banking, and finance industries.
- *Standard Directory of Advertisers.* Data on more than 25,000 companies that spend more than $75,000 annually on national or regional advertising; includes annual sales, number of employees, product names or brands, officers, name of advertising agencies, and media used. A second volume identifies more than 62,000 trade names.
- *Standard & Poor's Register of Corporations, Directors, and Executives.* One volume of data on 55,000 corporations, including names, titles, and functions of officers, directors, and other principals, and descriptions of products and services; one volume of data on individuals serving as officers, directors, trustees, and partners, including their business affiliations, colleges and years of graduation, and fraternal memberships.
- *Thomas Register of American Manufacturers.* 25 volumes of detailed information on products and services, including specifications and drawings, and on the companies that supply them.

The following periodical indexes will refer you to articles about companies, industries, and corporate officials you are researching:

- *Business Index.* A microfilm index to 500 business and financial periodicals, *The Wall Street Journal, Bar-*

rons, and the business section of *The New York Times*, plus 1,100 other general and legal periodicals, government reports, and books.

- **Business Periodicals Index.** Index to 275 periodicals.
- **Predicasts F&S Index.** Indexes 750 financial publications, business newspapers, trade magazines, and special reports for information on mergers and acquisitions, new products, and technological developments.
- **Standard Rate & Data Business Publications Directory.** Publications are grouped by subject area; useful for identifying the business publications that cover a specific field.
- **Wall Street Journal Index.** Monthly index to the final Eastern edition of the newspaper. Part I of the index covers corporate news, indexed by company name.

Observation: One extremely useful publication is *The Wall Street Transcript*, a weekly newspaper that includes reprints of speeches by corporate officials to financial analysts, abstracts of corporate annual and interim reports, and industry overviews.

Now, go beyond the literature. "Find out as much as possible about the company, the way it operates, the way it makes decisions," urges Riley at American Airlines. "If, for example, you're interviewing for a position in sales, find out how they judge success—is it just on the numbers, or on the basis of new accounts? Does the organization want, say, four cold calls per week? You'd need contacts in the organization to find out something like that."

Reread that last sentence: "You'd need contacts in the organization to find out something like that." That is yet another persuasive argument for constantly working to build the broadest possible network. Sometimes contacts provide names, and sometimes they provide information.

Be creative, and you'll think of other information sources. For example, John Marino, a Massachusetts-based independent recruiter who has handled assignments for computer companies such as Digital Equipment Corp. and Data General, suggests that an applicant for a job with a computer company talk to that company's vendors.

It also helps to know about the parameters of the job, so you can focus your presentation. Ask the recruiter who placed the ad to tell you as much as he or she can. If you have samples of the kind of work you do, ask which ones would be appropriate to have with you.

And call the company to find out what the regular business hours are. If you'll be at an upper level of management, your hours may very well be longer. But they certainly won't be shorter. And if you know before you walk in that the hours are 8:30 to 4:30, not 9:00 to 5:00, it's just one more fact that enables you to talk intelligently about the company.

Organize the information you find

To keep track of the information you find on companies where you are going to be interviewed, make up a "Company Profile/Interview Sheet," using the headings on the next page. Start filling out your form as soon as you have an interview scheduled, but note that you can't complete it until after the final interview. Additional information that will be needed is explained in Chapter 6.

Observation: You may not need information for every category. It will depend on the job level you're reaching.

Here are the headings for your Company Profile/Interview Sheet:

- Company name in full (include the Inc., Corp., or Co.; be sure to note whether or not the company uses a comma before that term and whether it uses an abbreviation or spells out the word.)
- Address
- Telephone number
- Fax number
- CEO
- President
- First Vice President
- Second Vice President
- Treasurer or Comptroller
- Other officers
- Directors (names and affiliations)
- Annual sales
- Number of employees
- Products/Services (include categories and the brand names within those categories)
- Names and addresses of divisions or subsidiaries
- Important facts about the company you have learned from your research (include article titles and sources, so you can say, "I read thus-and-such about your company in an article in *Fortune*," rather than "I can't remember where I read it, but . . .")
- Job title for which you are interviewing
- Job requirements that you already know about
- Questions that you want to ask the interviewer
- Date and time of interview
- Name and title of interviewer

You will continue to add information to your profile until after your final interview with a company. See Chapter 6 for the rest of the headings.

Identify your key strengths and achievements

"The purpose of a resume is to get you an interview"—
more conventional wisdom. But if that's true, then what's
the point of going into an interview and simply repeating
your resume? "As you can see, I worked on the Zinger,
Zowie, and Fabbo projects." If the interviewer can
already "see" that, why are you sitting there? Unless you
can amplify what's on the resume, you're wasting everyone's time.

**What does this particular interviewer want to
know?** Certain projects, achievements, responsibilities,
or personal skills are bound to be of greater interest to
this prospective employer than to another. You'll have
some idea as to which ones are relevant to this position if
you've done your research thoroughly. Focus on those,
and reconstruct them in your mind in as much detail as
possible.

Ask yourself: What was the objective of the project?
The timetable? The constraints? Who originated it? Who
was in charge? What resources—people, materials—
were required? Where did you fit in? What was the
outcome? What do you wish had turned out differently?
What would you do differently next time so that the
outcome would be better.

Observation: You will need answers to questions like
this. Wait until you're one-on-one with an interviewer to
try to formulate them, and you'll blow it. The time to
come up with these answers is now.

Be as thorough as possible at this stage. Write down
as much as you can remember about the experiences and
examples that illustrate your abilities and achievements.

You'll have ample opportunity to shape all that information into a more succinct format when you plan your presentation, and again when you rehearse.

Review your personal history

"Go back and really revisit your own life," says Korn/Ferry's Foster. "It sounds silly, but make sure you even know where you went to elementary school." How could that possibly be important? Foster explains that the interviewer might notice on the resume, for example, that your early years were spent in Pittsburgh, and remark that his brother had attended elementary school in Pittsburgh before the family moved away. "Which elementary school did you attend?" he asks, looking for a connection, and you reply, "Gee, uh, well, I really don't remember."

Says Foster, "We're looking for 'bridges.' But if we don't have the facts about ourselves, it's hard to build those bridges."

Be sure, too, that you know the date on which you started and ended each previous job, and the name of the person to whom you reported, Foster cautions. "If you don't know that last detail, you not only can't build a bridge, but your record is suspect: 'He can't remember who he worked for?!' That's a red flag."

Remembering and clarifying such details also helps ensure that there's agreement between what your resume says and what you write on an application. Even if what looks like a lie turns out to be a simple case of poor memory, the discrepancy will work against you.

Caution. Discrepancies are trouble spots that you might be able to overcome. But outright lies will do you in. Disregard the occasional tale of an untrained "surgeon" who was in practice for many years before being found out, because no one had ever bothered to check his references. Companies do check backgrounds, and will find out if a candidate never attended a school from which he or she claims to have an MBA. Don't be tempted.

Plan your presentation

Several interview questions are listed below. Some of them are questions that research has shown are likely to be asked in an interview; some are actual questions asked by companies to which we spoke.

Unfortunately, finding out the interview questions ahead of time is not the same as getting a copy of an exam in advance. It does not enable you to look up the right answers, because there are no "right" answers. The only answer that is right for you is one that is based on what you yourself have accomplished and experienced.

But you can develop effective personalized answers if you know what those answers should convey, and what concerns they should address. Thus before you begin to prepare your answers, you need to know what prospective employers really have in mind when they ask specific questions.

What are interviewers looking for?

The interviewer makes a decision on the basis of three areas, says Paul Stuhlman, senior outplacement consultant with Personnel Corp. of America, Norwalk, Connecticut, a management consulting firm specializing in human resource disciplines. These are the interviewer's concerns:

- **Experience.** Certainly the interviewer wants to know whether or not the candidate has the experience needed to enable him to handle the new position successfully. "To answer that concern," says Stuhlman, "the candidate must find a way to communicate his experience as it relates to solving the problems in his area of expertise. That means talking about specific accomplishments: 'Here's the problem; here's how I approached it; this was the result.' A manager, in particular, should be able to show a quantifiable result."
- **Chemistry.** The next concern is whether or not there is a good "fit"—does the interviewer want the candidate on the team? Is his style one that the company would be comfortable with? To respond to that concern, Stuhlman says, a candidate "must be sensitive to the style of the interviewer—but you can't be a person you're not." (For more on how to respond to the style of the interviewer, see Chapter 5.)
- **Enthusiasm.** "We all agree that enthusiasm is very important early in one's career," Stuhlman says, "but it's just as important in a management interview. An interview is similar to a sales call. All of us as buyers find it appealing if a salesperson tries to help us. A good salesperson must be enthusiastic about doing so—but it must not be put on; it must be controlled and appropriate."

If you need any additional proof that you'll be judged on much more than your on-the-job accomplishments, look at the situation at IBM. At that company, every effort is made to promote from within. In Chapter 1, Morgenroth was quoted as saying that one advantage of that practice is that "we already know the person's work history." Yet when an employee is being considered for another position within the company, he or she still goes through the interview process. Why?

"We get more into behavioral characteristics, to determine people's motivation, their responses, their flexibility in accepting work assignments," says Morgenroth. "We ask probing questions, phrasing them to get at the characteristics we're trying to assess. We'll ask people to talk about something they've done, and ask, for example, 'What was your reaction to that, considering what was involved?' We're looking for a 'can do' attitude. Where one person sees a problem, another may see an opportunity—the challenge of trying to be innovative, creative, of doing something new."

Guidelines for effective answers

Agreed—you can't look up the answers to interviewers' questions. But you can, and must, prepare your own answers to the questions you think you might be asked. As you do so, you may find it helpful to keep in mind these guidelines, as suggested by Joan Learn:

- *Be concise.* "People tend to go on too much," she cautions; "they ramble." Get right to the point and answer the question in two or three minutes. (Ways to keep your replies to the correct length are explained below.)
- *Quantify.* You have to pack a lot of information into those two or three minutes. Do it by using numbers, not adjectives. Don't say, "We saved a substantial amount of money"; specify the dollars. Don't say "a

significant increase"; mention a percentage. Don't say you've had experience supervising "large groups"; say exactly how many people you mean.

- **Structure your answers.** Start with an introductory statement that gets right to the point and also states your strength. If you're asked what your management style is, for example, you might open with, "My management style is participatory, and I think that makes me an effective leader."

Don't stop there. That alone will come across as a canned answer and will hurt, not help. Go on to give an example that proves what you have just said. Lead into it with, "For example, there was one time that . . ." or "I recall a project I worked on that required me to . . ."

And wrap up with either a summary statement or a feedback question—depending upon how much you already know about the requirements of the job: "That kind of approach helped me to build a strong team that could always be depended upon" or "Do you think that that skill would be valuable in this position?"

Anticipate the questions you will be asked

There are dozens of questions that interviewers can ask. But certain questions—or types of questions—will come up in every interview, in one form or another. Although you could never be prepared for each and every one, not being prepared for the standard ones is bound to reflect badly on you.

"Think about the things you'll probably be asked," says Morgenroth, "things like 'Why are you interested in this position?' 'Why do you think you are competitive?' 'What can you bring to this position?' You shouldn't let yourself be surprised or stymied by any of those."

The following are several questions that you are likely to be asked, with suggestions for what you should—and should not—include in your answer.

"Tell me about yourself"

It's the oldest question in the book—one that recruiter Marino calls a "plain vanilla question"—and consequently it will be asked, in one form or another, in almost every interview. Yet, "Most people flub the answer because they don't know where to start," says outplacement consultant Stuhlman. His suggestion: "Draft an outline of the major points you want to get across. You may want to communicate your major strengths, or the types of organizations you've worked for, your significant accomplishments, the direction you're interested in pursuing. Be sure to include all the things that make you unique or special."

If you've identified the accomplishments you want to highlight, and have reviewed your personal history, you're off to a good start on this one. But you can't be sure how much of that the interviewer wants to hear. So you need to prepare a summary that, like all your answers, runs two to three minutes. (You'll be amazed to discover how much of your life you can summarize in that length of time.)

When you've given your basic answer, says Stuhlman, you can conclude with something like, "That was a quick snapshot. In what areas would you like more detail?" You're now giving control of the dialogue back to the interviewer—a good thing to do—and are also making it plain that you're prepared to handle whatever he or she asks for next. You've also created an opportunity to present more information about yourself without going on too long in a single answer.

"What are your weaknesses?"

"I have none" is an absurd answer, of course. The interviewer will not be impressed and humbled at being in the presence of such a paragon. Rather, he or she will think that you are poor at self-analysis, unable to accept criticism, unable to acknowledge faults, or unwilling to change or improve—none of which you want to convey. Nor can you say something as trite—and transparent— as "I work too hard" or "I'm a perfectionist."

Then how do you answer that question without tearing yourself down? "For most of us," Stuhlman explains, "our weaknesses are the flip side of our strengths, or our strengths carried to an extreme. For example, good leaders are sometimes insensitive to others. People who are visionary, sociable, warm, and open can overlook details. But people who are analytical, methodical, and logical can be indecisive."

During the self-assessment process, you identified your major strengths and skills. Study them to see which ones you possibly carry too far. Be honest with yourself—you will need this answer. Then turn your insight into a response that shows that you not only have acknowledged the problem but also have worked to overcome it—and that becomes another strength.

Example: Stuhlman suggests one such answer: "Because I'm a strong leader, I have to be careful that I don't come down too hard on people. In my earlier years as a manager, there were times when I might not have listened to my staff as carefully as I should have. So now I stay on my guard to be sure I don't let that kind of thing happen again."

Example: You might also try something like this: "Because I'm so concerned about quality, I used to find it hard to delegate. But I've learned that by getting to know my staff really well, I can match people with projects and delegate effectively."

You will, of course, have to support such statements with specific examples.

Observation: Note the careful wording that puts the weakness into the past: "In my earlier years . . . there were times . . . ," and "I used to . . ."

"Why are you looking for a job?"/"Why did you leave your previous job?"

Note: "Why did you lose your job?" is handled separately, below.

These two questions are actually asking the same thing: What is it that makes you dissatisfied and sends you looking for greener pastures? The interviewer is attempting to determine your motivations, and also anticipate what the company can expect from you if you join the staff.

So, of course, you want to put a positive cast on the answer even while you adhere scrupulously to the truth. "I hate [or,hated] my work," although possibly true, will not endear you to the interviewer. Ditto for "My compensation is an insult."

At one time, "There's no opportunity for advancement" or "I'm looking for a challenge" might have been an acceptable euphemism for "I hate my work." But no more. Interviewers are smarter these days and recognize a canned response when they hear it. Anyone can read that answer in a book and parrot it at the appropriate time.

Thus you need to answer the question in a way that only you can. What kind of advancement do you have in mind—supervising a larger group of people than you have in the past? Being named a vice president? Moving into a corner office? What challenge are you looking for? What do you *want* to do that you cannot do in your present job and think you could do in this one? What problem are you aware of in this company that you would like to help solve? Why should the interviewer want to hire you, rather than one of the 38 or 138 other applicants for this job?

If, in fact, you are looking for a job with a better compensation package, why are you worth it? What are you doing in your present job, what are you contributing, for which you are not properly compensated? Why will you be worth that compensation at this company?

Recommendation: Rather than resenting each question as another hurdle you must jump, try to see it as one more opportunity to sell yourself, to illustrate your strengths.

Why did you lose your last job?
There is no longer any stigma in being fired or laid off if it was strictly for reasons of the economy or a restructuring. If it has just happened to you for the first time, you may find that hard to believe: "There has to be some reason why they decided to let me go." If it has happened to you several times because of an upheaval in your industry, you may find it even more difficult to accept. But look around you, see that you are part of a crowd, and *believe* that what happened is no reflection on you.

In fact, the interviewer probably is more accepting of

your dismissal than you are. He or she is aware of employment (and unemployment) trends, and may even know of what is happening in your own company. Thus, a brief explanation is all that's necessary: "As you may know, there was a reorganization at my company and my department was eliminated."

If it's appropriate, you may wish to add a positive statement: "My department head was very pleased with my work, and did check with other divisions to see if there might be an opening for me, but the entire company has tightened up."

If you were fired for cause, you lie about it, and the interviewer finds out that you lied—you're dead in the water. The only way to handle this one is to get a clear statement from your former employer of the reason for your termination, so that when your references are checked, you'll be in agreement. Then, when you're asked the question, give the agreed-upon reason, followed by a persuasive explanation of what you learned from the experience and how you expect to prevent a recurrence.

Caution: Although you should be honest, there's no need to shoot yourself in the foot. One interviewer was aghast when a candidate wrote on an application form that he had been fired for "insubordination." Was he bragging? Issuing a warning?

Unless his former employer intended to give exactly that explanation, and was going to try to prevent the man from ever obtaining another job in this field, surely they could have agreed on an explanation on the order of "difference of opinion on departmental objectives." Then the candidate might have been given an opportunity to explain, and his former employer might have been contacted and asked for his views. As it was, the interviewer was turned off and the candidate was simply eliminated from the running.

"Why do you want to work here?"

Do not permit yourself to say "Because I need a job." In fact, this is where your research pays off. There is a reason why you either approached this company on your own or let a search firm or agency arrange the interview. What do you know about the company's stability, reputation for innovation, or respect for the individuals in its employ? What is it about the job that appeals to you— intrigues you, challenges you, excites you? If you can't answer those questions convincingly for yourself, you certainly can't answer them for the interviewer.

"Why have you changed jobs so often?"

If you have been a job-hopper, stress that you were able to accomplish quickly what was required of you in each position, and that new challenges did not appear. Give one or two specific examples of what your responsibilities were in a particular job. Then turn your response into a plus by mentioning what you were able to accomplish in what length of time, and the variety of things you learned on each job—thus demonstrating the range of your abilities. Marino's suggestion: "I'm looking for the opportunity that will keep me in one place for a while."

Summarize by asking the interviewer a question about the challenges that this job can provide. Because every interviewer thinks that challenges abound in his or her firm, your response should offer reassurance that you will not be so quick to leave this time.

"Where do you hope to be in——years?"

A few years back, one of the questions favored by hiring managers was, "Well, young person, if you come to work for our company, where would you like to be five years from now?" The appropriate response was, "I'd like to have your job, sir [or, ma'am]!" Such a response supposedly revealed initiative, commitment to the company, a long-term career strategy, etc., etc., etc.—and, rumor had it, clinched the job for many eager candidates.

Today, interviewers recognize that that answer is indicative only of the ability to memorize the responses that presumably are expected, and an inability to think for oneself. Moreover, says Executive Coach Kate Wendleton, "In this economy, asking what you see yourself doing five years from now is pretty stupid; people have to do more short-term thinking."

That doesn't mean, however, that you won't face an interviewer who asks that stupid question. If it happens to you, skip right past the canned, outmoded answer and say that although you recognize the need to be flexible in these uncertain times, you also don't intend to just sit back and wait to see what happens to you next. Thus what you aim to do is . . .

Recommendation: Be sure that your preparation includes the questions you don't want to be asked. You'll be much calmer knowing you can handle them if they're sent your way—which they very well may be.

By now, you may be starting to think that interviewers' questions are designed to cause candidates to fail. Not at all. The objective is to make a good match between candidate and job—and isn't that what you want, too? The interviewers' goal is to uncover as much information as they can to enable them to predict your chances of succeeding on the job.

For example, interviewers at S.C. Johnson & Son, Inc. (also known as Johnson Wax), in Racine, Wisconsin, try to gather relevant information by asking questions that are "behaviorally based," says Thomas J. Newman, director, training. In other words, the questions can be answered only with a description of what an individual actually has done. The rationale for this approach, Newman explains, is that "past behavior predicts future behavior. If you have done something in the past, I can find that out during the interview, and I would expect you to be able to do it again. But if you haven't done something in the past, why would I have any reason to believe you can do it in the future?"

By no means does this suggest that only candidates with experience identical to that required by the job are considered. In fact, Newman stresses that this approach gives recent graduates or people coming in from another industry a chance to prove their potential by encouraging them to discuss experiences that reveal what they can do.

For example, an interviewer might ask an applicant to describe an instance when he or she started something from scratch and carried it through to completion. The individual might talk about having planned a conference that went off without a hitch. Or a college student being interviewed for a sales position might be asked to describe a situation in which he or she had to persuade someone to agree to something. "The student could even talk about persuading the dean to let a group hold a beer party," Newman quips, if the anecdote reveals a capability and makes a point.

To stimulate applicants' thinking, Newman suggests that they think of a star: Describe a

Situation in which you had to perform a

Task. What was the

Action you took, and what were the

Results?

S.C. Johnson's interviewing technique is based on a concept called "targeted selection," which was formulated by Development Dimensions International, in Pittsburgh. Although Johnson so far is using the technique only to interview and hire office support staff, it is "usable at any level," Newman says; "the behavior-oriented questions apply to any job."

Recommendation: Keep the *STAR* acronym in mind when you are formulating the answers you want to give in your job interviews. It can help you to be certain that you have included all the necessary elements when you relate examples of what you have done.

Surviving stress interviews

Aren't they *all* "stress" interviews? Have you ever been interviewed for a job you really wanted and not felt a certain amount of stress? And many so-called stress interview questions are pretty much part of the standard repertoire. Still, don't confuse the stress you feel anytime you're on the line with a "stress interview."

What makes a stress interview different is not so much the questions, but the inhumane conditions. There are tales of the interview being held in a room that is uncomfortably warm or cold, an interviewer sitting in front of a sunny window so that the candidate was forced to squint into the glare, several interviewers hurling a volley of questions at the candidate—even of a candidate being urged to "pull up a chair" when the chair was in fact nailed to the floor, to see if the thwarted individual would assume that he was paralyzed by his own fear.

What if the horrendous happens to you? "Not too

many companies use stress interviews," says Learn. Still, you could be faced with one. If you are,

- First, realize that this is a deliberate attempt to see how you handle pressure and the unexpected. But because it isn't totally unexpected for you, you're not thrown off balance.
- Slow yourself down a bit, think before you react or respond, and show that you are in control and unintimidated: "There's a glare from that window and it's very distracting; do you mind if I move the chair a bit to one side?" "This chair seems to be stuck. Rather than waste your time while I deal with it, why don't I just sit right here and we can proceed." But don't remove your jacket, or even ask permission to do so, even in a sweltering room; mop your brow if you must.
- When the questions finally start, you'll recognize them, and you'll be prepared to answer them. But don't rush in. The most common stress-induced error is answering a question that's different from the one that was asked. If you ask for clarification, or pause briefly and look thoughtful—but not panicked—you'll buy extra seconds and also show that you're treating the process with appropriate seriousness.

Observation: If repeated or unexpected stress will be a major component of the job, a stress interview may be a valid way to test your ability to handle the job. But if you won't be subjected to stress, if this is just the company's way of conducting a killer interview, think carefully about whether or not you would want to work for a company that uses such methods.

The types of questions asked in stress interviews are not necessarily the mark of a sadist. Companies do need to know if you can tolerate a reasonable level of stress. Interviewers at Johnson Wax, for example, determine an individual's "stability of performance under pressure and/or opposition" by asking a candidate to "give me some examples of when your ideas were strongly opposed in a discussion. How did you react? What was the result?"

Numerous career guidance books go into great detail presenting sample questions and suggested ways to answer them. One that is particularly comprehensive and well thought out is *Knock 'em Dead with Great Answers to Tough Interview Questions* (see Appendix). Do look at these books, but realize that none of them is gospel. You don't need to—shouldn't even try to— memorize the answers they present. The value of such books is in stimulating your thinking. Find the approaches that are comfortable for you, that work for you. Then mold them into your own style and personalize them with examples from your own life.

Rehearse, rehearse, rehearse

Actors rehearse their lines and their moves. Athletes practice their skills. Salespeople practice their presentations. When you go on a job interview, you are performing, you are competing, you are selling yourself. To go in cold and try to wing it is an unacceptable and unnecessary risk. You have to rehearse.

You have been conducting a self-assessment continually—in very general terms before you even started looking for a job, in job-specific terms once you had an interview scheduled. We stressed that in those earlier stages, you should note everything that you could remember and that seemed relevant about your experiences, because there would be a right time to make all of it more succinct. This is the time.

As you were reading the sample questions, you no doubt began to develop your answers, working from your head or your self-assessment notes. Now's the time to focus on that development. Pick out the relevant experiences and write out answers to the questions, giving special attention to those you consider difficult.

Next, read one of your answers aloud—tape record it, if possible—and time yourself. Use either a stopwatch or a clock with a large second hand: The seconds matter.

You want your answer to be two to three minutes long. What did you have on the first try—thirty seconds? Ten minutes? You may be very surprised to find out how far off—in either direction—you are.

Now it's time to start rewriting. Add or subtract information as needed to achieve the right length. Read your answer aloud again, timing it. Rewrite, reread. Rewrite, reread. Repeat the process for each answer you prepare.

Hard work? You bet. Time consuming? No question. But if you find it difficult and time consuming to develop these answers when you're alone, what would it be like if you tried to do it on the spur of the moment, when you're face-to-face with an interviewer? "Impossible" may be the first word that comes to your mind.

Observation: If you have impressive credentials, why sabotage yourself by being unable to communicate them to an interviewer?

Outplacement counselors and communications consultants frequently use role-playing practice at this stage, and videotape the sessions so job hunters can critique themselves. If you are doing this on your own, it's a good idea to try to find someone with whom you can do your own role play, and who can coach you. "Role play at least a dozen times before you do the first interview," Korn/Ferry's Foster urges. "You have to know your story."

Avoid memorizing each answer word for word. Your responses should sound natural, conversational. If you memorize, you'll sound stilted, as though you're reading from a script. The interviewer will be unimpressed, and possibly even a little suspicious: Why can't she remember her own life?

You can remember it, of course. The practice is intended to help you remember the *right things* at the *right time*, rather than simply rambling aimlessly.

Carry a cue card. If you're still concerned about being able to remember everything on the day of the actual interview, you might try a tip recommended by Wendleton in her book *Changing Jobs* (see Appendix). She suggests writing the following information on a 3″ x 5″ card that you carry with you and review just before the interview:

- The main reason this employer would want to hire you
- Your major strengths—experience, credentials, personality
- Two key accomplishments to support your interest in this position
- An answer to the main objection—if any—that the employer may have
- Your main reason for wanting to work for this company

Observation: Note that this cue card includes some general information that you want to convey in any interview, along with some job-specific statements.

Consider some interviews a rehearsal. If you're

lucky, your first interview will not be for the job you really want. Thus it can be a kind of "dress rehearsal." This doesn't mean you don't have to take it seriously. Do the very best you possibly can. Then, critique your performance afterward. (You should do this after every interview, of course—more about this in Chapter 6.) Identify your weak spots, determine what you need to do to strengthen them—and go to your next interview a much more polished performer.

"Anyone can, through practice, become outstanding in a candidate interview," says Foster. Yet few people do the necessary practicing. That's encouraging news, considering how tough the competition is and the importance of finding something that will distinguish you. Many of your competitors won't practice. But you will—won't you?

Prepare yourself mentally

Looking for a job has never been high on most people's lists of fun things to do. It's hard work: You feel as though you're on trial every time you meet with an interviewer, and you face rejection repeatedly.

Job hunting is especially difficult if you're not doing it by choice. If, for example, your company has had to let you go after many years, you may be feeling betrayed: "How could they do this to me?" And if you've spent your entire career with a company that recruited you right out of college, and have never actively looked for a job before, the job hunting process may be alien and even seem a little demeaning.

It is important to acknowledge those negative feelings, but then try to put them behind you. "If a person was with one company for twenty-five years, it may take four to five months before he or she becomes forward looking," cautions Wendleton. "The longer you focus on the past, the longer your search will take."

To help defuse those negative thoughts, Fuchs Cuthrell's Dinah Day suggests a three-part strategy she calls "exercise, affirmation, and dumping and doing."

- *Exercise.* Do so three times a week, Day advises, and "not alone." Get outside, even if all you're doing is fast walking. Regular exercise enables you to "bring some energy, life, passion, and attitude" to the way you carry yourself and wear your clothes, she says.
- *Affirmation.* Keep a self-image journal: Every day, write down ten good things about yourself. You may find this difficult to do at first; Day points out that men tend to list only eight things, and women only six. Another gender difference: When Day asks people to pay themselves a compliment when they're on camera, "a man may say, 'That's an interesting request' or 'I hadn't thought about that.' But women always start the response with 'What I don't like about myself.'" Women should be alert to that tendency and fight it. If you're asked about your strengths, be sure that's what your response reveals. Otherwise, you are unnecessarily calling attention to your weaknesses—and you're not answering the question you've been asked.
- *Dumping and doing.* On the days when things are especially rough, you need to be able to call someone on whom you can "dump"—to whom you can say "I don't want to do this interview," or "I hate the suit I'm wearing—it's not right for the interview." The person you call at a time like this isn't necessarily your best friend, Day says. "In fact, it probably shouldn't be;

your best friend will make excuses for you. You want someone who will support you, who will say, 'What do you need? What can I do to help you?' That's why it's so important to have a mentor." You might even call someone you've just met through networking, she says; the person will be honored to be considered a source of support.

After you dump and get the support you need, do what you must: Go to the interview, focusing on the many positives you have to offer. To complete the process, call the person back afterward and report on the outcome. "The person will be hanging out for you all day," she says.

See your own success

Going into an interview demoralized will hurt your chances. You won't be at your best. But if you go in feeling like a winner, you'll project that confidence, that "can do" attitude that Morgenroth at IBM says is so important.

One way to "psych" yourself up beforehand, and thus improve your performance, is by visualizing a successful interview. Don't think it will work? Then try this: Think of all the things that could go wrong on the day of the interview. You sleep through the alarm, a heel comes off your shoe, your zipper breaks, your car won't start (or you miss your train), you forget your samples . . . you get the idea. Aren't you starting to feel uneasy as you envision all the disasters that *might* happen?

Now turn it around. Imagine waking up five minutes early because you're so excited about the opportunity to present yourself to a particular interviewer. You've rehearsed thoroughly, and you know you have something special to offer this company. Picture yourself handling the interview smoothly, confidently, and the interviewer nodding and smiling when you leave. . . .

Visualizing success doesn't guarantee that you'll achieve it, of course. But the attitude it creates certainly improves your chances.

Prepare yourself physically

The way you look affects the way you feel, and the way you feel affects the way you look. You have to get everything right if you want it all to work together. Especially when you're going for a job interview, you want to look and feel like a person who is competent, confident, prepared, and has it all together.

To be at your peak on interview day, be sure you've had enough sleep. Drink as much coffee as you need to keep yourself alert—but not so much that you experience the digestive problems coffee sometimes causes.

Pay careful attention to your grooming. Body odor, dandruff, clothing that isn't spotlessly clean and properly pressed, or scuffed shoes will all work against you. Some children and college students express their individuality by being sloppy. If you do get a job despite these shortcomings, you'll find yourself consigned permanently to the lower rungs of the organizational ladder.

Observation: Many women carry a spare pair of hose in their purse or briefcase, so that a run during the day won't ruin an otherwise perfect outfit. Men scheduled for job interviews late in the day might want to carry an extra tie in case the one they're wearing acquires a spot at lunch.

Posture is important. Slouching implies that you lack energy and self-esteem. With good posture, you'll look like a leader and project a more confident, self-assured image.

Look at yourself in the mirror. Do you look energized and ready to win? If not, take a few deep breaths. Stand with your weight centered buoyantly over the balls of both feet, rather than sunken into your heels. To stand tall with comfort and flexibility, don't throw your shoulders back military style.

Wrap your physical package in appropriate clothing. An all-purpose conservative outfit of the type described in Chapter 1 will take you to almost any interview. If you are a candidate for an upper-level job, however, you may wish to find out more about what is appropriate at a specific company. Photographs in the annual report will be of some help. If the company is nearby, you could spend a few minutes in the lobby, or sitting in your car in the parking lot, observing the way others are dressed. If all this smacks a little too much of foreign intrigue for you, or if the company is too far away to make it practical, you may simply want to get some inside information from—who else?—one of the people in your network.

Dressing according to a particular situation does not mean that you are compromising your own individuality. It means that you are being respectful of the people with whom you are meeting—and wisely trying to advance your own cause. A female sales training consultant who favors trendy clothing—pants outfits, lots of black, striking jewelry—on her own time, says that when she calls on Wall Street firms, she wears a conservative suit. Her objective is to make a sale, not a personal statement; thus she presents an image that will please the prospect.

Example: Do respond to subtle differences that you may be aware of within your own field. For example, architects are generally more flamboyant in their dress than engineers, and both groups sense that difference. One engineer, aiming to look as though he would fit right in, wears what he refers to as his "architect shirt"—one with bold stripes—when he is interviewed at an architectural firm. But he never wears such a shirt for an interview at an engineering company, where, rather than fitting in, it would stand out.

Caution: Even if the interview takes place in the dog days of summer, a woman should wear hose and closed shoes, not sandals or open-toed pumps. A man should wear a jacket, and keep it on during the interview unless the room is so warm that the interviewer suggests he remove it.

Keep your image consistent. For many jobs, you'll need to appear for more than one interview. That means you may want to have more than one interview outfit. But don't wear anything that's radically different from what you wore the first time, cautions Day. "A woman should wear an outfit that's similar. A man should wear either the same suit with a different tie, or the same tie with a different suit." Nor should you make a major change in your hairstyle, or grow—or shave—a beard or mustache between interviews. You want to look like the person they remember.

Remember, though, that it takes more than image. As important as physical appearance is, don't make the mistake some people do and think that you can sell yourself with image alone.

Example: A middle manager arrived at a job interview in a fine suit that was entirely appropriate for the company where he was interviewing. Opening a top-quality briefcase, he produced an engraved business card, along with a professionally produced resume and copies of articles he'd written that had been published in top industry journals. When the interviewer began to ask questions about the manager's objectives, however, the manager laughingly stated that he wanted to make a lot of money and ultimately run a company, and he thought that this company might be the right place to do it. In one instant, his lack of preparation took him right out of the running. In fact, the elegance of his external image made him look even worse, because it had primed the interviewer to expect much more.

Get help if you want it

If you are terminated, your former employer may arrange for an outplacement firm to work with you. This service generally includes full office support plus extensive counseling: personal assessment, guidance in the selection of career paths, and assistance throughout the job search. "We teach people a process they can use for the rest of their lives," says Joan Learn of the outplacement firm The Greenwich Group.

If outplacement isn't provided, you don't have to go it alone. There are numerous training, networking, and support groups, plus counselors and coaches who will work with you one-on-one. Such groups and counselors are listed in telephone directories. You'll find them in consumer yellow pages under such headings as "Career and Vocational Counseling" and "Image Consultants" and in business-to-business yellow pages under headings such as "Image Consultants" and "Personnel Analysis and Consultation Service."

A number of coaches and counselors are also listed in the *National Business Employment Weekly* (NBEW), published by Dow Jones & Company (publisher of *The Wall Street Journal*), which is available at newsstands and by subscription. NBEW also reprints help-wanted advertising from the regional editions of *The Wall Street Journal*.

Caution: Be aware that there are no licensing requirements or professional standards for most of these groups and consultants. Anyone can call himself or herself a career consultant, and it can be difficult to distinguish between the competent professionals and the charlatans. Check credentials—look for some kind of affiliation with an established entity, or ask for references—before wasting your time or investing large sums of money.

This is yet another instance in which someone in your network may be able to make a recommendation.

Are you ready for the interview at last? Not quite. Your final preparation will be done after you arrive at your target company. You'll then be able to walk into the interview and give a job-winning performance.

5

How to Succeed
in Job Interviews

This is it—your chance to show an interviewer how good you are, to present yourself as a competent and confident professional.

But you still need to put the finishing touches on your presentation. That's why you should *arrive at the interview fifteen minutes early*, and use that extra time to your advantage.

As soon as you arrive, ask the receptionist if there is somewhere for you to hang your coat; you don't want to have to deal with it when you go into the interview. Then stop at the rest room. Take a quick look at your cue card, and run that information through your mind once more. Then check yourself out in the mirror: Hair combed, not windblown? Tie straight? No lipstick on your teeth? Jacket properly aligned? Inhale and exhale deeply, stand tall, and smile at yourself approvingly.

Back in the reception area, chat with the receptionist. How long has he or she been with the company? What's it like to work here? Spontaneous responses to questions like these may give you some insight into the work atmosphere. You might even try a question like "Have they been interviewing a lot of people for this job?" to get an idea of how much competition you have. Or "Have they hired a lot of people lately?" as an indication of growth. Watch out if you get a response like "Well, actually, they've just let a lot of people go": It may be a revolving-door operation.

Observation: This conversation is also a good opportunity to warm up your voice and be sure you're comfortable with the pitch and the volume. If you sit silently for fifteen minutes, the first sound when you finally open your mouth might be squeaky, or crack a bit, or be either too loud or too soft.

Notice the reception area, both to learn about the company culture and to find something of interest that could be the basis for opening small talk with the interviewer. Are the walls covered with awards and honors won by the company? Is the decor formal and severe, or are there whimsical touches? Is there a painting or piece of sculpture worthy of comment? Or a striking view?

Then you hear the receptionist say, "Mr. Crane will see you now." Your fifteen minutes are up. Pick up your briefcase in your left hand—you'll need your right one free for a handshake. Now you're ready.

Who's the "real" interviewer?

In many large corporations, your first interview will be with someone in the "Personnel" or "Human Resources" department. And this, recruiters agree, is where many candidates make their first mistake. They think that this is not a "real" interview, and that it is either demeaning or a waste of their time.

Interview error: Snubbing Human Resources. The human resources interview is not unimportant, not a mere formality or an opportunity to ask about company benefits. It is, in fact, the initial screening. But "fast trackers, entrepreneurial people, or salespeople often don't want to see someone in Human Resources," says executive recruiter Berardi. "They don't realize that the person in Human Resources has a lot of power in the company."

On more than one occasion, says independent recruiter Marino, a candidate brought in to see him would protest, "John, I thought my appointment was with the hiring manager." When Marino pointed out that the interview with him was part of the process, the candidate would demand abruptly, "What do you want to know?"

Mistreating the Human Resources person is "one of the most foolish mistakes a candidate can make," says Marino. "People don't realize how much influence he has on the final decision. And that kind of behavior also shows that the candidate doesn't know enough to treat all people with respect."

The interview with Human Resources counts for a lot at American Airlines, too. Hiring managers simply do not have the time to see every candidate because there are so many: Of 1,200 MBA graduates who were interviewed in 1990, 120 were hired; and of the 600 to 700 management candidates interviewed, 200 to 300 were hired. Thus Human Resources evaluates "chemistry" and "fit." The successful candidates then go to hiring managers to be interviewed about the technical aspects of the job.

During the Human Resources interview, says American's Riley, "We're trying to find out if you're a decent human being." That is hardly insignificant. Interviewers also want to "get a feel for the person's commitment to work, because we work long hours here. So we'll ask how you go about planning your day, or what you do in your spare time."

There may also be questions that relate to the work itself. Says Riley, "I might ask a candidate to describe a high-tech job, to see if he or she can do so [in such a way that] I can understand it. People who work as consultants may have to explain things to a nontechnical person, and must be able to speak in layman's terms."

Observation: Clearly, the Human Resources interviewer may have just as much to say about the final decision as any hiring manager. Thus a candidate should treat the individual, and his or her questions, with courtesy. Moreover, this means that all the guidelines in this chapter apply to a Human Resources interview as well as to an interview with a hiring manager.

Make the right first impression

By now you know that you'll be judged on much more than just your professional skills. Interviewers also evaluate the content and style of your presentation—what you say as well as how you say it—your attitude, and your appearance. That evaluation starts the minute you come face-to-face with the interviewer.

Interview errors: The wimpy handshake, the shifty eye. "First impressions are critical," says Marino. "A lot of decisions are made in the first thirty seconds. How does the person look—is his tie on straight? There has to be a solid handshake—not wimpy—and good eye contact."

Fortunately, that critical first impression is one of the easiest things to get right. You know your appearance is fine; you've just checked it out. Look the interviewer straight in the eye, smile, and then, as you extend your right hand for a handshake (you've kept it free—remember?), say, "Hello, Mr. Crane, I'm Leslie Prince. I'm pleased to meet you."

Observation: At one time, there was some debate on whether or not a woman should extend her hand for a handshake. "Those days are gone forever," says Wayne R. Phillips, director of The Executive Etiquette Co., Taunton, Massachusetts, a corporate training and consulting firm that specializes in business protocol. Not only is it now accepted, and expected, that a woman will shake hands, but "the person who extends a hand first is the hero."

Interview error: Sitting down without an invitation. After the greeting, wait to sit down until you are invited to do so: "Please have a seat, Mr. Prince." Usually, the interviewer will indicate where you should sit. If you are given a choice, however, take the chair that puts you in the best position to maintain eye contact and that enables you to sit up straight. Sink into soft cushions and you may have trouble projecting your voice.

An additional pointer from Phillips: Unbutton your suit jacket as you sit down, but rebutton it when you stand up.

Caution: Smoking at the interview is hazardous to your job prospects—unless, of course, you are interviewing with a tobacco company. The only time you might consider smoking is if the interviewer is doing so and offers you a cigarette. Even then, think about it. Would you rather have your hands free for reaching for papers, taking notes, and so on? If so, you'll rarely go wrong with a simple "No thanks" that's free of any judgmental vocal overtones.

How to pass your "chemistry test"

Interviewers are concerned about chemistry—the way you interact with them. You are now about to take your "chemistry test." You'll pass with flying colors if you establish rapport with the interviewer. Clues to help you do so are all around you. Just look, and listen.

Look at the surroundings. You've already done that in the reception area, and may be able to make an opening, positive comment about something you noticed there. Check for the same kinds of things in the interviewer's office: citations, artwork, memorabilia, view. Your objective is to show that you are *interested in* and *aware of* the surroundings, and are *favorably* impressed.

What you don't want to do is open with a remark about what a tough day you had, or the traffic you had to fight your way through to get to the appointment, or how slow the elevators are in the building. Such comments are not innocuous; they will hurt you in several ways. Why? They are negative, indicate excessive self-concern, cast the prospective employer in an unfavorable light, and clearly suggest that you would not be happy working here: "If he was so bothered by a long wait for the elevator when he's coming for a job interview, he certainly wouldn't want to have to endure it five days a week."

Listen to the interviewer's tone. You can't be phony, and you can't be something you're not. Yet to ignore the

97

interviewer's manner entirely and proceed in your own way, even when it is quite different from the interviewer's, will make you appear rude and even combative.

Interview error: Not responding to the interviewer's signals. "The interviewer is directing you, and you should be open to the pacing," says Fuchs Cuthrell's Day. Thus you should modulate your voice so that it is not much louder or much faster than the interviewer's. (The opposite is more difficult: A soft-spoken person may not be able to talk in a way that he or she considers "shouting"; a deliberate and thoughtful speaker may not be able to start rattling off answers.) Watch the wisecracks if the interviewer is serious and straight-faced. But lighten up if the interviewer is jocular; sit there impassively and it will appear that you either have no sense of humor or are not very bright.

Observation: If you spot the clues but are unable to respond to them, or if you find it uncomfortable to adapt to the style of a particular interviewer, then the chemistry is wrong for *you*. It does have to work both ways. This may not be the company, or the job, for you.

Listen for the hidden messages. Establishing rapport is not something that you do once, and then move on. Good rapport must be maintained throughout the interview. Here again, careful listening is the key. "People only half listen," Marino points out. "They need to understand not just the question, but where the interviewer is coming from. Where does he see the critical issues?" Marino gives an example related to the computer industry: "If the interviewer says the project is late, and the software is not complete, and two of the engineers don't have enough experience in the language of that program, you can reply with the strengths you have that he's lacking. Even though he didn't ask the question," Marino says, "he's telling you he has a problem or need."

By picking up on that hidden message, you have demonstrated that you have more than technical proficiency. You have shown yourself to be a perceptive and responsive person, one who can spot problems and jump right in to solve them.

Body language travels two ways

In addition to the verbal messages—both spoken and unspoken—people who meet face-to-face are communicating via body language. You need to pay attention not only to the messages you send, but also to the messages you receive.

Sending messages. You send a major message with your eyes. By maintaining eye contact, you show that you are interested in what the other person is saying. You also indicate that you are telling the truth and thus are comfortable looking the other person in the eye—something that is especially important in a job interview.

But Consultant Day maintains that "too much is made of eye contact. It's inappropriate to have a staring contest." Her point is well taken: You don't want to fix another person in your gaze in a way that makes you both uncomfortable. Thus, as the interview progresses, you may wish to look away on occasion to break the intensity.

You can continue to show that you are paying attention and do understand what is being said, however, with a smile or nod of agreement, a "Yes" or "I see" or "Mm-hmm."

Your posture can also convey alertness and self-confidence if you sit slightly forward in your chair, rather than leaning against the back. And both men and women should cross their legs at the ankle, not at the knee, Phillips advises: "Crossing your leg at the knee is a very casual approach, but there is nothing casual about this situation. This is not someone's living room."

Caution: Nervous gestures can transmit messages you never intended to send. Fidgeting, adjusting a tie, scratching an ear, or laughing at inappropriate moments have been identified by psychologists as signals that a person may be lying. Women sometimes fiddle with their hair when they're nervous; the action is "unempowering," says Day. It may also be seen as flirtatious. Similarly, a man who nervously flips his tie is inadvertently making a sexual gesture.

Receiving messages. You receive your first message from the interviewer during the greeting. Does he or she stand up and lean across the desk to shake your hand, keeping the desk as a barrier between the two of you? This is not a sign of hostility, but it does suggest greater formality than coming around to sit beside you at a conference table. You'll show that you received that message if you maintain a formal manner when you speak.

Notice, too, how the interviewer reacts when you are speaking. Is he or she smiling and nodding, or frowning? Looking out the window? Tapping fingers impatiently? "If you're rambling, the interviewer will have an exasperated look on his face," Marino warns. It's time to refocus and get your answer back on track. Summarize as quickly as you can: "Once I had presented those options to the staff, they realized why it would be to everyone's advantage to put in the extra hours on this project, and we made our deadline. So I think that I should have no problem keeping your project on schedule."

Observation: It shouldn't unsettle you if the interviewer takes notes. In fact, it should encourage you that you have said or done things that are worth remembering. On the other hand, if the interviewer does not take notes, you may wish to repeat or refer back to points that you especially want to have remembered.

The interview as self-sell

There are strong parallels between a sales call and a job interview. In an interview, you are selling your own capabilities, but the steps are much the same as they are for a person selling a company's product or service:

- *Prospecting.* Just as salespeople study a market to identify likely prospects for their companies' offerings, you have been looking for companies that might employ you.
- *Qualified leads.* When you respond to an employment ad or apply at a company identified by an executive recruiter, you are following what salespeople call a "qualified lead"—this is a company that has revealed a need you might be able to fill.
- *Cold calls.* When you approach a company on your own, however, you are making a "cold call"—you are not certain that a need exists, but it is a reasonable probability.
- *The interview/sales call format.* In both cases, the applicant/salesperson must first establish rapport. Then, through a skillful blend of "probing" (asking questions), "presenting" (giving examples of your qual-

ifications), and handling objections, you determine whether or not a match is possible.

- *Rejection.* Yes, this is part of both processes. Salespeople don't make a sale on every call. And you will not be offered a job by every interviewer you see. Some factors are beyond your control, no matter how thoroughly you prepare. But the ability to bounce back from rejection and keep on going is just as necessary for you as it is for a salesperson.

- *Closing the sale.* When a salesperson identifies a need and presents the product or service that can meet that need, he or she will close the sale. And you will get the job.

Observation: The most successful salespeople are the ones who think of themselves as consultants. Rather than trying only to "make a sale," they are looking for ways in which their offering can help the prospect and meet needs. To keep the parallel going, try thinking of yourself not as a person who really needs to get a job, but as one who has something of value to offer the interviewer. That attitude will be reflected in your "presentation," and you'll come across as more positive and more competent.

Watch your verbal mannerisms

The "like" and "y'know" that young people sprinkle throughout their speech annoy many listeners. If you're guilty of such usage, make a conscious effort to eliminate those meaningless and distracting syllables from your speech before you start going on interviews. Also work on jargon and on any "ums," "ahs," and "ers."

Two university professors recently completed a study of speech habits that revealed that speakers who are more knowledgeable about their subject matter use fewer of those "um" and "ah" types of pauses. Thus interviewers are likely to perceive you as uncertain of what you are saying if you speak haltingly. But you'll come across as authoritative and in control if you speak smoothly.

Observation: Using a tape recorder during your pre-interview rehearsals will make it easier for you to spot, and work on, these problems.

As for industry jargon, overuse can work against you rather than making you appear authoritative, warns Executive Coach Wendleton: "A lot of people can't explain to the outside world what it is they do." She tells of one manager who was skilled in the operation of a communications system that he and his colleagues always referred to by its name. But when asked to explain it to an interviewer, he could only say, "Well, it's a . . . a *system*."

It's especially important if you've spent many years in one industry and are now looking in a different area not to expect an interviewer to be fully conversant with your terminology. Be able to explain what you do in plain English.

Keeping the interview in balance

An interview is a dialogue between interviewer and candidate. Neither side should do all the talking. Thus it's a mistake to sit silently while the interviewer outlines the basic responsibilities of the job, assuming that a resume is all you need to tell your story. But it's also a mistake to get so carried away selling yourself that you neglect to ask any questions of the interviewer. You need to aim for a balance between the two.

How do you tell them what they didn't ask? Selling your qualifications is no problem if the interviewer asks all the right questions. You've prepared detailed, clear, persuasive answers. But what if the interviewer doesn't ask about something that you particularly want to talk about—doesn't give you the opportunity to sell yourself? How do you tell your story?

Recruiter Foster suggests two possible approaches. You might use a questioning format, such as the following: "You never asked me what color the pencils are—is that important?" Or you could make a statement: "There are a few things you haven't asked me about that I'd like to share with you. They are A, B, and C."

Note that the first approach is somewhat tentative, asking permission, and the second approach is slightly more forceful. Your choice will depend on the tone that has been established in the interview—how formal it is—and how controlling the interviewer has been.

A major mistake that job candidates make is trying to take control of the interview, so you don't want to come on like gangbusters. But you should be sure that you've had a chance to present all the strengths that you believe are pertinent to this job.

If the interviewer is a nonstop talker, and you're concerned about offending him or her if you interrupt, Berardi suggests that you segue in with "One of the things I found out about your company . . ." That keeps the focus on the interviewer initially, and doesn't make it appear that you are trying to take away the spotlight.

Observation: Members of minority groups need to be especially aware of the questions that interviewers have neglected to ask. The reasons for interviewers' avoidance, and ways to deal with it, are discussed elsewhere in this chapter.

Interview error: Letting the interviewer ask all the questions. As you are selling yourself, don't lose sight of the fact that you, too, are buying. You need to find out as much as you can about the job requirements and working conditions in order to decide if you really want this job.

"The most important questions an individual needs to ask the potential employer are the qualifying or quasi-close questions," says PCA's Stuhlman. "Ask the hiring manager the requirements of the job, the problems, the business issues that need to be solved or accomplished. Ask, for example, 'What will you expect the new person to solve in the first six months?' Such questions really help you understand the organization's needs."

To the job requirements, problems, issues list, Marino adds the following: "What kind of people have been in this position? Where are they now—were they fired? Did they quit? Were they promoted? What makes people successful in this job?" He also suggests asking questions about the management style, the company's marketing plans—whatever you need to know to help you decide if you want the job.

If the position is a new one, you might ask why it is being created. Is it taking some responsibilities from other people? With what other positions will it interface?

What? No questions about the benefits package? Certainly you do need to know about benefits. But those questions come much later. Asking them too soon gives the distinct impression that your only interest is in what the company can do for you. And that does not position you as an applicant who can help the company solve its problems.

Observation: Asking questions is part of your self-sell. It's one more way to show that you've done your homework and that you're genuinely interested in this particular company, this particular job. If, for example, the company has been involved in a merger, says Wendleton, you could ask the hiring manager, "How is the merger affecting your division?" But if the interviewer refers to the merger, she says, "and you don't know what he's talking about, you obviously aren't really interested in working at that company."

As your questions are answered, take notes. Astonishingly few job candidates take notes during an interview. Here's why you should:

- *You'll need the notes to refresh your memory.* You'll be interviewing at more than one company, and probably seeing more than one person at each of those companies. There's no way you can remember everything each person tells you. And without all the information at hand, you can't make an informed decision about the job.
- *It's further evidence that you're interested in the job.* Interviewers know that you'll see many people, and can't possibly remember everything everyone tells you. If what they're telling you isn't important enough for you to want to remember it, do you really want the job?
- *It helps keep you calm.* The act of writing can dissipate a lot of nervous energy, and can keep you focused. It also eliminates the worry that you might forget something important.
- *It relieves the intensity of eye contact.* You do want to break the stare occasionally, but don't want to let

your eyes roam about the room as if you're bored. Looking down at your notepad solves the problem.

- *It sets you apart from other candidates.* Because so few candidates take notes, interviewers tell us that they tend to remember those who do. The more memorable you are, the better: As long as what makes you memorable is professional.

Fielding off-limits questions

Title VII, the civil rights law that prohibits discrimination in employment, also plays a role in the interview process. Interviews are considered tests under Title VII and thus may not result in discrimination against a candidate based on that person's race, sex, creed, national origin, or color. Questions are considered discriminatory if they do not relate to any bona fide occupational qualifications of the job.

For example, a female job applicant who was asked whether she would get pregnant and quit, or if her husband would mind if she had to "run around the country with men," recently won a sex discrimination suit against the interviewing company. Some other questions that interviewers are forbidden to ask include the following:

What they can't ask women

- What are your plans for marriage?
- What are your plans for childbearing?
- What arrangements can you make for your children during working hours?
- Would you be inconvenienced by travel?

- Would you be inconvenienced by night work?
- How would you feel about supervising men?
- Is your husband likely to be transferred to another location within his company?
- What would you do if your husband were transferred?
- Can you sell as aggressively as a man?
- Do you think you can leave your family problems at home and concentrate on the job?

What they can't ask anyone

- Do you live alone or with someone? (This could be considered an invasion of privacy.)
- Do you go to church regularly? (This could be viewed as religious discrimination.)
- Are you a Republican or a Democrat? (This could be an invasion of privacy.)
- Were you ever arrested? (Most states prohibit this question, but usually permit the interviewer to ask if the applicant was ever *convicted* of a crime—especially if the job involves security or confidentiality. Interviewers may also ask if you can be bonded; convicted felons can't.)
- What type of military discharge did you receive? (This could be discriminatory because minorities have a disproportionately higher percentage of dishonorable discharges than whites.)
- Do you have any physical disabilities or handicaps? (The interviewer *may* ask if the applicant has any disability that would interfere with his or her performance on the job.)

Although most interviewers today are aware of what kinds of questions cannot be asked, occasionally an inappropriately worded question is asked in all innocence. Of course, there are also interviewers who ask such questions intentionally, thinking they're not likely to be found out because few applicants would bother to file a suit.

How should you respond to an off-limits question? You have three choices:

- *You can refuse to answer.* If you say something like "You're not allowed to ask that" or "That's an illegal question," you've put the interviewer on the defensive, regardless of his or her motivation. And you've pretty much ruined your chances for employment with the company.
- *You can parry.* Asking, "Does that have any bearing on the job?" or "How would that affect performance of the job?" might make the interviewer realize that he or she has inadvertently strayed across the line. But this is also a risky approach, says PCA's Stuhlman. "You're taking a combative stance, and that does nothing to improve the rapport you're trying to build."
- *You can show your insight into the question.* A question that has no bearing on the qualifications for the job may nevertheless indicate an interviewer's concern about your ability to handle the job. The smoothest way to reply is with an answer that relieves that concern.

  For example, a woman who is asked whether or not she plans to have children might reply, "If you're wondering whether or not I can commit to the job full-time, I can assure you that I can. My plans for a family will be influenced by my career progress, and I would hardly leave just as opportunities are opening up for me."

You may feel that you're yielding to pressure, or not defending your legal rights, if you respond in this way. The reality is, however, that only this kind of response will keep you on a good footing with the interviewer.

Observation: If you're asked several pointed, off-limits questions, you can be pretty certain that the interviewer is not speaking "in all innocence." You'll be seeing a clear pattern of an intent to discriminate, and you most likely would not want to work for the company in any case. But you'd be wise to continue with the interview, rather than storming out. And continue taking notes, but without making a special point of doing so. If, after the interview, you feel that you have grounds for pressing charges, you'll have your support in writing.

Minority candidates and unasked questions

In trying *not* to be discriminatory, interviewers may hold back their questioning in a way that actually works to the detriment of minority candidates. So says Monroe "Bud" Moseley, senior associate at Isaacson, Miller, Inc., Boston, an executive search firm at which about one-third of the staff and one-third of the new hires are minority candidates. "A majority interviewer might 'walk on eggshells' to avoid sensitive subjects or confrontation," says Moseley, who is himself African American.

What's wrong with that? The problem is that an interviewer might think that a minority candidate is more show than substance, but not know of any nondiscriminatory way to find out the reality. For example, explains Moseley, an interviewer might have doubts about a candidate's credentials because of stereotypical attitudes, but not want to voice those doubts. "An interviewer who's majority might think, but not want to ask, 'How did you, a black person, get into Harvard Business School? Are you really that good, or was this affirmative action?' Or they might wonder about your relationships with peers—how did you manage lunches with clients?"

Minority candidates need to realize that such concerns exist below the surface, and address them. "Help the interviewer understand the depth of your responsibility," Moseley urges. "Explain the range of your contributions in a defined way. For example, don't just say that you were responsible for a budget of a certain size. In some companies, they just give you the budget, but in others you have to defend it or decide when you'll request more. If you did that, say so. And let the interviewer know if you maintained vendor relations or customer relations through direct contact, that you determined places for dining or hotels in which to stay. Show the interviewer what you have faced, what you have achieved.

"People of color are not accustomed to blowing their own horn," Moseley points out. But in a job interview, "humility is not a benefit."

When you're interviewed over a meal

A job interview may be conducted over a meal if you're a finalist for an upper-level position. The interviewer may want to observe you in the type of social setting that is part of the job responsibilities. Or the interviewer may be conducted over a meal simply as a scheduling convenience. In either case, you now have another set of concerns to deal with: your dining etiquette.

Business Protocol Consultant Phillips, who is author of *The Concise Guide to Executive Etiquette* (see Appendix), suggests ways to deal with the major concerns in this situation:

- *Arriving at the restaurant.* If you arrive before the interviewer does—and you should never be late—wait in the reception area, rather than allowing the maître d' to seat you. If the interviewer is someone you have not met before, try to obtain a description of the person to facilitate the meeting; the most effective way is to speak by telephone that morning and tell each other what kind of clothing you are wearing. Should you recognize the interviewer before he or she sees you, do walk over and introduce yourself.
- *Being seated.* When you are shown to your table, "There's inevitably a preferred seat that is pulled out," says Phillips. "Usually, that seat is for the female. But in this case, the pulled seat is for the person of authority—the interviewer." Protocol calls for you to wait until the interviewer asks you to be seated. The interviewer might motion to the preferred seat and ask you to take it. If so, accept it. "Oh, no, you take it" or any other kind of protest is inappropriate.
- *Coping with the napkin.* Open the napkin and place it on your lap immediately after being seated, says Phillips, and "don't tuck it into your shirt or belt." If you need to leave the table at any point during the meal, place the napkin to the left of your plate, not on your seat. Do not refold the napkin; simply take it by the center and pull it into an elongated shape.
- *Ordering a drink.* Alcohol is not a good idea because it

may keep you from thinking as sharply as you need to at this time. But you should order something from the bar, whether juice or a soft drink, "so that your host's drink doesn't arrive unescorted," says Phillips.

- **When and what to order from the menu.** Let the interviewer indicate when it is time to order—"Shall we take a look at the menu?" Choose a mid-priced entree, unless the interviewer specifically recommends a higher-priced dish that appeals to you. And make your choice fairly quickly, so that you can get back to the business at hand.

  Caution: Avoid all finger foods, anything that is difficult to eat—such as lobster in the shell and pasta, which may splash when it is twirled. Some salads are risky, too: The dressing may drip or cause a woman's lipstick to smear unattractively. And certainly do not experiment with an unfamiliar dish. Your best bet is something simple that you can eat without paying much attention to it.

  If all these prohibitions make it seem as though you aren't going to have much of an opportunity to enjoy the food, realize that that is as it should be. "You're not there to engage in a culinary delight," Phillips points out. "The meal is simply a vehicle for the discussion."

- **Opening the conversation.** Again, let the interviewer lead the way. But if it becomes apparent that he or she is waiting for you to speak first, do not launch into business immediately. There should always be a preliminary conversation. Make a positive statement about the decor of the room, Phillips advises, or comment on a recent cultural event in the city: "It's good to be alert to the arts." Whatever your choice, "stay on safe subjects—and never say anything negative about the food."

- **When to talk business.** If no business subjects have been brought up after about fifteen minutes, you may turn the conversation in that direction with a statement like "I understand that your firm has been in this location for twenty-five years. Where was it before that?" The remark is not intrusive, but does send the message that you are ready to get down to business.
- **Ending the interview.** Wait for a signal from the interviewer, who may refer to having to leave for another appointment, or words to that effect. If the signal comes before you've had a chance to say—or ask—everything that you wanted to, say something like "I do have one short question—do you have time for it now, or would you prefer that I send it to you?" That way you have indicated your interest in the job, but have also acknowledged the interviewer's schedule.

Handling objections

Confident, well-prepared salespeople welcome objections. In fact, Samuel W. Smith, vice president of sales for National Trade Productions in Alexandria, Virginia, refers to objections as "the salesperson's best friend." Why? Because responding to them gives the salesperson one more chance to sell, one more chance to strengthen his case. Thus he encourages his salespeople to "solicit objections, then knock down every one of them, like bowling pins." They do so with questions like "Is there anything you're concerned about?" or "Is there anything else I can help you with today?"

Continuing the analogy between a sales call and a job interview, it should be apparent that you can benefit by finding out if the interviewer has any doubts about your suitability for the job. You can then resolve those doubts. Marino suggests trying to bring objections to the surface by asking questions such as "Am I a strong candidate for this position?" or "Do you think I'm qualified?" or "How did I do against the other candidates?" Says Marino, sounding much like a sales vice president, "You want the opportunity to combat the objection. If you don't find out about the interviewer's concerns, you walk out of there losing.

Observation: A common objection—"You appear to be overqualified for this position"—may be voiced more often as shifting organizational structures make it necessary for some people to seek jobs below their previous level. Marino suggests that a candidate can turn that objection into a benefit with a response such as the following: "I'm interested in the job. If I am overqualified, that means my manager can download some responsibilities to me. And as the department grows, I can grow along with it. In the meantime, you're getting more for your money."

Talking money

This is one of the thorniest parts of job interviewing. Should you ask about the salary, or should you wait for the interviewer to bring it up? Should you get a fix on the salary range early in the interview, to decide whether or not to continue the discussion? Should you be honest about your present—or most recent—compensation?

You'll be in a stronger position if you can delay any discussion of compensation until you've had a chance to sell yourself, to show the interviewer what you would be worth to the company. Thus, avoid mentioning money in the initial interview. If the interviewer asks early on, "What salary are you looking for?" try to postpone answering. Joan Learn suggests a response such as "I'd really like to find out more about the job first—the job and the fit are what's most important to me now." It's the rare interviewer who will insist on pinning you down to a number immediately.

But if not immediately, then perhaps eventually. The consensus is that if asked about your present or most recent compensation, you should give the true number, not an inflated one. Learn suggests, however, that you reply, "My compensation is [or was] . . ." and include the entire package of bonuses and perks, not just salary.

Stating your salary objective is more complicated. As Marino points out, "The interviewer has an unfair advantage here." Name a number that's below the range the company had in mind, and you've just cost yourself money—and maybe even the job. As a recruiter for a Fortune 500 firm told a disappointed candidate with otherwise excellent credentials, "Around here, they figure if you'd work for that little, you mustn't be as good as you look."

But a number that's too high may also cost you the job. Try to toss the question back to the interviewer: "What have you budgeted for the position?" Do everything you can, short of antagonizing the interviewer, to postpone the discussion to the best time for it. . . .

The best time to talk about money is when the company is ready to offer you the job. By then, you'll have a clearer idea of what the job responsibilities are, and what compensation you'd consider appropriate. You'll also have some leverage because the company will have decided that it wants you.

How to blow the interview

Throughout this chapter, we've called your attention to a number of "interview errors." Unfortunately, those aren't the only ones. There are a number of missteps that job applicants can make, through ignorance or carelessness, that can cause them to lose out on an opportunity for which they may have been qualified.

The experts whom we consulted voiced the following do's and don'ts:

- *"Do* allow enough time for the interview," says Consultant Day. "Plan on at least an hour and a half." The reason? The interviewer may ask if you have time to see another person, and you want to be able to say yes—because the question indicates that the interviewer is favorably impressed. But, she says, don't give a reply that indicates you have all day.
- *"Don't* act as if you're not interested in the job," cautions Marino. "Often, when the choice is between two candidates, the hiring manager will say that one of them just didn't seem interested." You don't want to give the impression that you're desperate for the job, because that puts you at a disadvantage. But neither should you act "nonchalant," he says.
- *"Do* come into the interview with a positive attitude," says Morgenroth at IBM. "Be prepared to sell yourself. Understand that this is a dialogue and you are expected to contribute significantly."
- *"Don't* try to direct the interview," Marino warns. "If you try to take control, the interviewer will try to wrestle the control back."

- *"**Do** be very precise about what you accomplished,"* says Learn. "Have specific success stories, and intersperse them throughout the interview."

- *"**Don't** 'trash' your present employer,"* cautions Loretta Berardi. "If you're asked why you're unhappy in your job, say that there have been management changes, or that your opportunities for growth have been blocked."

- *"**Do** manage your references,"* Learn advises. "Keep them abreast of your campaign, and let them know what would be of interest for them to say. Otherwise, a reference could blow it for you." Find out, too, what your company is saying about your reason for leaving, to be sure that your stories match.

  Observation: This does not mean giving your references a list of the great things they should say about you. It means telling them which aspect of your responsibilities or which of your skills they should mention.

- ***Don't*** be rude to the secretary or receptionist in the Human Resources Department, or to anyone connected with the company. Riley says that American Airlines frequently flies job candidates in to its Dallas headquarters for interviews, booking them on flights on a space-available basis. "We've had people explode at the ticket agent when there was a problem with the flight," Riley says. "They'll say, 'Don't you know who I am?' We know who they're not going to be—an American Airlines employee."

Ending the first interview

We opened this chapter by telling you very specifically what would happen at the beginning of the interview. The end of an interview is much less clearly defined:

- You may be told immediately whether or not you got the job. But that's highly unlikely. There are almost certainly other candidates being interviewed. Also, the decision is seldom made by a single person. Thus you will probably be interviewed by others.
- If all went well, you may be asked on the spot to return for another interview.
- You may be told that someone will call you to schedule a follow-up interview.

Recommendation: If the interviewer is exceptionally vague, do ask what the next step in the process is, and when you can expect to hear from the company regarding that next step.

Then stand, reach for your briefcase, shake the interviewer's hand, and say, "Thank you, Mr. Crane. This has been a very informative conversation" or "I found this to be a very productive meeting, and I hope you did, too." Then, "I look forward to seeing you again"—whether you mean it or not.

In the outer office, tell the receptionist how much you enjoyed talking with her and that you hope to see her again.

And now—be on your way. You still have more to do.

6

Follow Up
and Wrap Up

It's a natural tendency to replay an interview in your mind, making judgments as you go—"I wish I had said . . ." "He looked pleased when I said . . ." "Would I really be interested in working on . . . ?"

Evaluate

Don't try to tell yourself that you shouldn't dwell on it—"What's done is done. I did my best, and now the next move is theirs." Instead, stay with this mental replay, using it to evaluate both your performance and the features of the job. Once you do that, the next move, the follow-up, will be yours.

But first, the evaluation. If you've used the Company Profile/Interview Sheet suggested in Chapter 4, you've already filled in the basics about the company. Now that you've had an initial interview, you can record what you know about the job and the working conditions by continuing your profile, using the following headings:

- Date and time of interview
- Name and title of interviewer
- Next step (second interview scheduled? to be scheduled? who is to call whom when?)
- Pluses of the job (responsibilities, working conditions, etc.)
- Minuses of the job (responsibilities, working conditions, etc.)
- Salary range
- Benefits (insurance coverage, bonus, vacation policy, etc.; you probably will have to wait until after a later interview to find out about them)
- What I did really well
- What I could do better
- What I did poorly (questions I couldn't answer, or didn't answer to my advantage)
- Objections I responded to
- Date of my follow-up letter
- Date and time of next interview
- Name and title of interviewer
  (. . . and so on until . . .)
  Final outcome (was/was not offered job, did/did not accept)

Filling out a Company Profile Sheet gives you an opportunity for thoughtful self-evaluation after each interview, in addition to a record of company basics and interview dates. What did you do well? Which of your answers got a particularly positive response from the interviewer? What did you do poorly? Were there any questions you were not prepared to answer, or did not answer adequately? What objections were raised by the interviewer? Do you feel that you addressed those concerns adequately?

Did any part of the interview make you uncomfortable? If so, think about it carefully and try to determine the reason. Is it something you could handle differently in another interview? Your objective is to identify any weaknesses that need to be corrected, so that you will do an even better job next time.

The next move is yours

Just because the interview is over doesn't mean that you can stop selling your qualifications. You not only can continue to sell, you must. Wendleton emphasizes that point when she says, "The only job-hunting technique that *works* is follow-up."

Follow-up reinforces your qualifications. It gives you a chance to say things you may have forgotten to say, or to correct things you wish you had said differently. And it distinguishes you from the other candidates—few people follow up. Thus it is a major influence on the decision maker.

How do you accomplish those desirable follow-up goals? With a carefully composed letter to the interviewer that includes these steps:

- *Repeat* your interview-closing remarks about having enjoyed meeting the person and finding the meeting "productive" or in some way beneficial or rewarding.
- *Review* your major strengths—the points you had on your "cue card."
- *Re-emphasize* your specific qualifications for this job.

Mention the issues or needs that the interviewer brought up, and the skills you have that will enable you to handle those issues or meet those needs.

- *Reiterate* your responses to any objections that were raised by the interviewer. Add any supporting material that you neglected to present during the interview.
- *Recap* the next steps—what the interviewer has said will happen, and when.

Note that each of the steps in your letter begins with "Re." The idea is that you are *repeating* and therefore *strengthening* each of the points that you want to convey.

Caution: Never use your company stationery for this follow-up letter. It sends a confusing message: "Why does she make a point of identifying herself with a company she supposedly intends to leave?" And it raises a sticky question: "Does she always use company stationery for her personal letters?"

Mail the follow-up letter within forty-eight hours of the interview, no later. The interviewer will be seeing other candidates and may not remember the details about you without a *reminder*.

If you don't get the job

Rejection hurts. You invested so much time and effort. You thought you did everything the experts say you should do. Yet you didn't get the job. But rejection is reality—for everyone. Says Learn, "Try to get interviews with twenty different companies if you want to get a job offer."

That advice isn't directed at you personally. The point is that *many* people can expect to be turned down by nineteen out of twenty of the companies at which they interview. Riley at American Airlines offers further consolation. "If you don't get the job, you can't feel bad about yourself," he says. "You are who you are, and you won't fit with everyone."

Don't let all that consolation turn into an excuse, however. There was a reason that you didn't get the job. Try to find out what it was. It may be something you could alter in future interviews.

Don't try to guess why. Come right out and ask the reason. Ask the executive recruiter. Or ask the interviewer if you are not working with a search firm: "I'm sorry you selected another candidate, because I really felt that I had something to contribute to your company. I'd appreciate it if you could tell me what the problem was."

Yes, they may be evasive. After all, it's hard enough to deny a person a job; why add insult to the rejection? But persist. You're likely to get a response if you say, "What you tell me might help me in future interviews." Who would want to deny you the opportunity to succeed elsewhere?

If you get feedback, use it. What you hear may be just one person's opinion. But if you begin to discern a pattern in the rejections, you'll know that there is something that you should try to correct. If it's something in your manner of presentation, you can work on that. If you're lacking certain skills or training, perhaps you should upgrade before continuing to pursue a job search in this field. Try to look at the comments objectively, as critiques you can use to your advantage.

If an offer is made

You'll have three choices if offered the job: Reject it, negotiate the offer, or accept it. Here are some points to keep in mind as you evaluate the offer:

- *The challenges and clout of the job.* The new job should permit you to move into new areas, sign off on a heftier budget than you have now, supervise a bigger staff, shoulder more critical responsibilities, or take on some other high-profile activities. Analyze the job's new duties before saying yes. One manager, for example, took a major promotion, only to find out that his new job involved writing memos and sitting in meetings half the day. It didn't satisfy his hunger to do something exciting. The new job was an advancement in terms of title and compensation, but the manager still felt significantly weakened.

  Observation: When you do things you love to do, you have energy and enthusiasm for them and can get ahead faster. Remember, too, that a title alone won't stand up to the scrutiny of future employers. They'll want to look at your specific responsibilities and achievements.
- *What you can do in the job.* You want to be able to advance, say, or to have the opportunity to cut costs, or reorganize the division into teams, or hire older workers and reduce turnover, or install new computers. Whatever your goals, unless the job offers room to grow—and promises future rewards—it is the wrong job.
- *The total compensation picture.* In addition to more

pay or better benefits, try to add some perks and termination protection with each successive job. They not only provide the proverbial umbrella for a rainy day but enhance your executive image.

• *The job's strategic value in your career path.* Even an excellent job may not fit in. For example, if you're now working for a major corporation, jumping to a small entrepreneurial firm may cut you off from a return to big corporate life. That may be fine with you—but do consider it before you make your decision. Having the courage to wait for the right job will give you the direction others lack. That will repay you richly in the end.

Observation: The time to exercise control over a new job is before you accept it. If one seems close to meeting your demands, but not quite there, consider whether negotiating the actual responsibilities will turn a tempting job into the right one.

"Usually there is little flexibility in changing the terms of the job," cautions Duke Foster. But he adds that it is possible. "If, for example, you said, 'In addition to being comptroller, I'd like to help out with investor relations,' that might make sense. Or, 'You mentioned that you hate to deal with financial analysts; maybe I could accompany you to meetings with them and help out. . . .'" This approach not only gives you a negotiating point for broadening the job responsibilities, but also can help you sell yourself.

Turning down the job
If the job does not meet your criteria, in terms of the kind of work you want to do, and the conditions under which you want to do it, of course you don't accept the

offer. But first, get the offer. Don't rush to end an interview, or stop in mid-process, unless you have serious reservations about the position and are certain that you're wasting everyone's time. Getting an offer is good for morale. And it also enables you to tell future interviewers, truthfully, that you've had other offers but they haven't been suitable.

But don't turn down a job you want, as a ploy, if the compensation is not to your liking. You may lose. You're on much firmer ground if you reply to the offer with "Thank you—I'm really interested in joining your company. But there is something I'm concerned about."

Negotiating the offer

You and the employer may each have your own agenda at this point. You may be trying to get as much money as you can—within reason, of course. And the employer may be trying to hire you for somewhat less than the job would pay. As PCA's Stuhlman explains, "Businesses do want to pay within the appropriate salary range, but below the midpoint, to give the person room to grow." At the same time, he says, management must consider "peer equity": They don't want to pay a new person more money than others with comparable responsibilities are already earning at that company.

Observation: One way to deal with the "peer equity" issue is to give you a title that's slightly different from the titles of others who have similar responsibilities. Employers sometimes suggest that on their own. If not, you should feel free to bring it up.

Think it over

Stuhlman advises against responding immediately when the offer is made. It's better, he says, to say you want to give it some thought. Then, do just that. Decide whether or not the offer is satisfactory, or if there are some terms you want to negotiate.

If you have an idea of what comparable jobs pay at this and similar companies, you'll know if your expectations, and the employer's offer, are reasonable. If both sides are operating within reasonable limits, and both sides think it will be a good match, the company should be willing to stretch its budget a little in order to hire you. But if the offer is well below what you know to be fair, and all attempts at negotiation fail, this may not be the job for you after all. You'll be starting off on a negative note, feeling that the company has taken advantage of you.

Caution: Don't expect that you will be able to correct an initial salary that's too low by winning substantial raises later. You'll constantly find yourself in an adversarial position with management. Besides, negotiating a higher starting rate is far easier than winning raises later on.

Are you giving up a bonus by leaving your old job? If so, get a signing bonus as compensation. Nail down your bonus structure with the new firm—for example, a prorated portion if you begin your employment at mid-year. Also, nail down a severance agreement if you can (see below).

If you're working with a search firm, the recruiter can play a key role in the negotiation process. "I encourage the candidate to think of me as the intermediary and talk openly with me," says Dick Barnes, president of Barnes Walters & Associates, an executive search firm in Milwaukee. "I call the candidate and tell him exactly what the offer will be. I'm listening for reactions, for comments like 'What do you mean, it's only $45,000?' or 'But I already get three weeks' vacation.'"

Barnes says that candidates sometimes keep such opinions to themselves. "But I need to know what they think," he stresses, "to get the expectations of both sides on the table. So I encourage candidates to call me back with comments or questions."

The real plus, says Barnes, is that the recruiter "is objective. I take the emotion out of it and try to keep both sides from blowing up." And that keeps the company–prospective employee relationship more positive from the outset.

Accepting the job

If you're satisfied with the company's offer, it's a simple matter to accept the job. "You don't have to ask for more just on principle," says Stuhlman.

Even in highly competitive times, don't act as though you're grateful for whatever you can get. After all, you presented your qualifications so effectively that the company decided it would benefit by having you, rather than someone else, on board. Acknowledge management's good judgment, and express your satisfaction with the offer, with a strong statement like "That's within my range" or "That's about what I had in mind. I'm glad we could reach an agreement. I look forward to joining your company."

Once the agreement has been reached, ask for a letter stating the day you are to join the company, your starting salary, and your other benefits. It's a simple formality that reduces the risk of confusion later on—and you can request it in just that way.

You may find that management at a small company is unwilling to give you such a letter, saying that it smacks of more structure than they are accustomed to. The reason for the refusal may be exactly what the person says it is; there may be no hidden agenda. Let your judgment and sensitivity guide you.

What about severance protection?

It's one of the harsh realities of today's workplace that even as you are joining a new company, and thinking excitedly about the opportunities and challenges ahead, you must also be thinking about what will happen if you are let go. Should severance protection be part of the package when you sign on?

Years ago, such agreements were limited to a select few megacorporations. No more. Today, even small firms will grant them if pushed—and if they want you badly enough. What's more, nobody holds such a request against you.

If you have been offered an executive position, and want to negotiate a severance package, be guided by the following checklist from Howard Pines, president of BeamPines, a human resources consulting firm in New York City:

- *Job duties.* Get a detailed description, and an agreement that the severance pact will be triggered if the duties change radically—if, for example, the company tries to make you quit by giving you menial tasks.
- *Compensation.* Get your stock option package in writing, including the amount, date, and what you keep if you leave the job.
- *Gap-free medical coverage.* Your new firm's medical coverage should remain in effect until *new coverage*

begins at any subsequent job—not just until you begin work at another firm, where coverage may not begin at once.

- **Vesting.** Ask to be vested from your first day on the job. This allows you to claim any and all employer-matched funds in your account, even if you leave after a short time.

- **Perks.** Are company cars, club memberships, etc., part of your severance package? For how long? Have it spelled out.

- **An arbitration clause.** Get an agreement that any post-employment disputes will be settled by arbitration, rather than in court. Arbitration is cheaper and faster—and arbitrators are more sympathetic to the little guy.

- **A "successors and assigns" clause.** Smaller companies are sold all the time. Be sure that any new owner will be bound by your written agreement.

- **A signature from a company officer.** If the only signature is that of someone other than the CEO, president, or other officer, the company may try to declare your agreement invalid if disputes arise.

- **A reasonable "noncompete" agreement.** You want one that won't jeopardize a subsequent job. Agree not to take confidential information or hire away employees, but balk at not working for a "competing firm" without being given a list of companies. Otherwise, you may have trouble working for anyone.

- **A favorable relocation clause.** It should provide for moving costs to the new assignment—and back to your original location if the job doesn't work out—plus the taxes you'd have to pay on moving expenses that are considered taxable income.

- **Outplacement.** Get an outplacement services clause

that will ensure you one-on-one outplacement counseling with a firm of your choice. Or write a list of acceptable firms into the agreement.

You've been offered a job you want, and you've accepted. All the details have been worked out to everyone's satisfaction. Good luck in your new job—and keep right on networking. Now it's your turn to grant courtesy interviews.

II

MASTERING
MEDIA INTERVIEWS

7

The Media Interview
as a Win-Win Situation

Media interviews terrify many people. Even top executives, proficient in their fields and outstanding in their human relationships, break out in a cold sweat at the thought of being under the TV lights. And the sight of a reporter's notebook or tape recorder can cause a normally voluble person to dissolve into a series of "uh," "er," and "well . . ."

Why the terror? Many reasons. The idea of being "onstage," of "performing," can be discomfiting. There's also the fear of the unknown—the unfamiliar situation, the uncertainty as to what the interviewer will ask. But, just as with job interviews, if you're organized and prepared, you can approach the interview with confidence.

Then, too, there's the perception that the interviews are mine fields. One misstep, and a loaded question may detonate in the face of the unsuspecting interviewee.

"There's no need to be intimidated," says media training consultant Carol Jaber, president of Jaber & Company Communications, New York City. "Unless it's a real adversary-type show, they're not out to get you." With the exception of "trash TV" and its equivalents in other media, what most journalists are out to "get" is a good—and accurate—story. Journalists probe in order to uncover the truth, whatever it may be.

Observation: Rather than being a threat, a media interview is a valuable opportunity to put yourself, your company, and your products or services before the public. If it weren't, why would public relations practitioners constantly be petitioning the media on behalf of their clients?

Take a look at both sides of the media interview and you'll see that, in fact, it has the potential to be a win-win situation.

How you can win

Good press is at least as effective as good advertising—and a lot less expensive. An interview is an opportunity to

- Promote good news—a new or improved product or service, a major corporate development.
- Defuse bad news—tell your side of the story.
- Position yourself as an authority or a reliable source.
- Convey a positive image of your company.

"The interviews that give people trouble are generally concerned with breaking news," says Jaber. "Consider questions about that news your opportunity to state the facts on behalf of your company or industry, and explain the situation or put things in a better light, especially if the news is tragic or controversial."

Taking advantage of media opportunities can pay off in several ways. They can help you

- Increase sales or revenues by letting more people know about your products or services.
- Reduce employee turnover and attract new applicants by building the company's image, and thus the prestige of being a part of it.
- Satisfy existing shareholders and attract new ones, again by building the company's image.
- Favorably impress industry observers by sharing your and your company's expertise—and possibly enhancing the industry's image in the process.
- Control damage when an accident, catastrophe, or a major quality or service problem casts your firm in a negative light. For example, Johnson & Johnson's quick response to the Tylenol tampering deaths in the eighties helped it to calm customer fears and later build back its market share. A company that experiences a fire or equipment breakdown that disrupts production could reduce complaints—and even build sympathy—by letting customers know, through the press, why they can't get what they want or need and when it will be available again.

Pinpoint your goal. One believer in the positive power of the media interview is Martin Yate, author of *Knock 'em Dead with Great Answers to Tough Interview Questions*. Yate is the subject of more than two hundred radio and TV interviews a year, by his estimate, as well as the occasional print interview. There are, he says, two basic reasons for participating in a media interview.

One reason is sales—"You want to sell this product, and so you'll plug it insufferably." The other is marketing—"You want to create top-of-the-mind awareness, to position yourself so that people will come to you in the future. So you may forgo the product plugs and concentrate on being a good guest, one who'll be invited back many times."

It's important to distinguish between the two and make your choice, says Yate. "You must decide if you just want to sell, and don't care if you're ever invited back, or if you want to be seen as a good guest."

Observation: Because interviewers so often get ideas from subjects covered by other interviewers, the benefits can snowball, giving you an even greater return on the time you invest up front.

You can lose heavily if you avoid the media. Some people consider members of the media intrusive and annoying, and avoid contact with them at all costs. But avoiding the press can be very costly. You lose the opportunity to gain favorable coverage when things are going well. And if trouble does strike, anyone you've slighted may be extra diligent in seeking and publicizing damaging information.

How the media can win

The media's objective is very basic. Radio and TV producers, and magazine, newspaper, and newsletter publishers, are looking for stories that will draw an audience, or readers. When they succeed, they sell ads and/or subscriptions, and make a profit. Simple as that.

Bringing it down to a more personal level, the interviewer's job is to get those stories. An interviewer doesn't pursue you because of any vendetta, but simply to keep his or her job. "Killer" questions are asked only because they might result in a better story. "If a journalist could write a story without interviewing people, why would he or she be running around making phone calls?" asks Jon Rosen, president of Impact Communications, a New York City company that specializes in news media interview training programs.

Help all those people do their jobs, and keep their jobs, and you will have allies. But how will they feel if you, in effect, endanger their jobs? And can you blame them?

Approaching the media

You don't have to wait for the media to come to you, to be able to take advantage of the opportunity for positive publicity. And you shouldn't, especially if your company is a small one that they might not easily notice.

Make the first move. Meet the editors who cover your industry for the daily and weekly newspapers in your area. Make a special effort with the trade papers; they can make or break you within both your industry and the financial community. Get to know the key players at the local cable TV and radio stations, especially those with all-news formats. They are frequently looking for stories to fill airtime.

Ask, "When's a good time to talk with you about . . . ?" Newspaper and broadcast news program deadlines tend to be close to press or airtime. Magazines, magazine-format TV and radio shows, and newspaper feature stories may be put together weeks or months in advance. You need to know newspeople's deadlines for two reasons:

- You want to volunteer information at the right time to get your story out when you want it out.
- When journalists are "on deadline," they aren't interested in anything other than important, late-breaking news. If you call to explore an idea then, you'll either be asked to call back or get only a perfunctory hearing.

Volunteer information. Once you've gotten acquainted with the various print and broadcast journalists, you can let them know when you have a story to tell. They'll appreciate your keeping them up to date, especially if they have space or airtime to fill. Be sure you alert the appropriate people, however. The producer or editor who wants to know about the development of a new packaging material may have no interest in the new plant you're building, and vice versa.

Don't limit yourself to news of your own company. Establish yourself as a reliable background source. If you're willing to provide insight into market rumors, industry trends, or maybe just a complicated term for a manufacturing process, it may pay off when the reporter has a chance to present your company in a favorable light at a later date.

But if you want to win big, you need to prepare. Chapter 8 will tell you how.

8

How to Prepare
for Media Interviews

A media interview, whether broadcast or print, can have
a lasting impact. What you said is on record, and will be
remembered. That, of course, is another reason that
people fear interviews. The solution: *Say only what you
want people to remember.* And the only way to do that is
to be prepared.

Refuse to be ambushed

Your telephone rings. You answer it. It's a reporter from
the leading magazine in your industry. She wants your
opinion of a product that one of your competitors introduced at a press conference yesterday. Her deadline is
immediate: She's revising a completed article to include
mention of this brand-new item.

Do you express your opinion? No. As Rosen points
out, "There's no difference between *60 Minutes* on your

doorstep and the reporter phoning you at your office. They're both ambush interviews. What's in it for you if you respond? Probably very little." You may even reap negative publicity if what you say isn't well thought out or you leave out a key point.

We will tell you repeatedly to cooperate with the media, to respect their deadlines, to be available when they call. All of that is in your own best interests. But don't sabotage those interests by giving an answer that you have not prepared—an answer that might be incomplete or make you sound uninformed, or be interpreted to mean just the opposite of what you intended.

Call the reporter back in half an hour, after you've had a chance to work up an answer. Call back in fifteen minutes if the deadline is really tight. Call from your car phone or an airport phone booth if you're on your way out the door and this is a person with whom you particularly want to cooperate. But hang up, think, and then call back.

Ambush interviews, which catch you totally by surprise, are rare—fortunately. Normally, interviews are scheduled, and you do have time to prepare your responses. In order for you to do so most effectively, however, either you or your public relations counselor should obtain some background information.

Initial briefing for broadcast interviews

To prepare for broadcast interviews, you need to know about the interviewer's style, the audience demographics, the format of the specific program on which you'll appear, and whether or not there will be other guests. The easiest way to begin gathering this information, of course, is to watch or listen to the program—several times, if possible.

How does the interviewer work? Some are very supportive of their guests. Some tend to joke a lot. Some ask extremely pointed questions. Some have a habit of being friendly until the person being interviewed allows his or her guard to drop, and then coming on with some stinging questions. Not knowing what to expect can be a tremendous disadvantage.

Studying the interviewer's approach helps you determine how aggressive you have to be to get in what you want to say. And if the interviewer uses a particular phrase, or tone of voice, before asking a touchy question, you can learn to spot that signal.

Example: Scott Simon, host of a magazine-format program on National Public Radio, frequently will say, in an especially supplicating tone, "Forgive me for asking this question" or "I hope you won't mind my asking you. . . ." as he moves into a question that the interview subject almost certainly *will* mind being asked.

Who are the viewers or listeners? You can find out by asking the production staff, or a contact person to whom you may be assigned. You can also deduce it from the time, day of the week, and community to which the program is broadcast, and possibly also from the network if it is on cable TV. Once you know the audience, you can work on gearing your tone and information to its members.

Recommendation: Watch or listen to several interview programs in addition to the one on which you're scheduled to appear, to learn how hosts or guests handle various situations.

What is the focus? Find out the topic of the program—or the segment on which you'll appear. Do ask if there will be other guests. "If they'll have someone else on, ask if they want the guests to take different viewpoints," Yate suggests. When a program wants to explore an issue, it will often invite guests with differing viewpoints in order to explore both sides. "If you're not expecting that," says Yate, "it can throw you off."

Initial briefing for print interviews

To prepare for an interview for a publication, find out about the journalist's credentials, the publication's readership, the focus of the article, and who else will be interviewed.

Who is the journalist? You may never meet the journalist face-to-face. If everything is handled by telephone, you may never really know who you're talking to—unless you make an effort to find out. Says one journalist, "I'm amazed at the number of times people answer my questions in detail without having any idea who I really am. I could be doing marketing intelligence for a competitor, or writing for a sleazy publication, for all they know."

The first time you're contacted by a journalist whose name is not known to you, and who has not been referred by someone you do know, run a check. Get the journalist's telephone number and call back, to see who answers. If it's a direct line, ask for the corporate phone number, or get it on your own. Call to find out if the person is actually there, or has ever been heard of. If the writer is a free-lancer and works at a different location, get the name of the editor for whom he or she writes and check with that editor. A true professional will not be offended if he or she finds out that you've gone through all those channels, but rather will be impressed by your thoroughness.

Who are the readers? If you are not familiar with the publication, you may want to know if it is local or national, and if the readership is limited to a specific field or function (secretaries? brand managers? training directors?). Ask for one or two sample issues so you can get an idea of the types of articles that are printed and the tone in which they are written.

What is the focus? The journalist will certainly give you an idea of the topics that will be covered. But you may also be able to get an advance copy of some of the questions that will be asked: Besides making it easier for you to prepare, it makes it more likely that the journalist will be able to use the material you provide. When you are contacted, the journalist may or may not know who else will be included in the article—it depends on who else he or she has already interviewed, how many others have agreed to be interviewed, and which ones in the latter group actually come through.

Observation: As the journalist talks with you and other people, new angles may appear that reshape the story. Thus, the final article may be different from what you and the journalist discussed initially.

"On the record" or "off"?

"Can I tell you something off the record?" you ask the reporter.

"Sure" is the reply.

But what agreement has been reached? What did you mean, and what did the journalist understand you to say?

A number of terms are used to refer to communication

that will not appear in the journalist's story, or if it does, will not reveal the identity of the source. The following definitions indicate what these terms usually mean. As you will see, however, the distinctions are not sharp. Your wisest course is to clarify the meaning of a term with each individual interviewer to be sure that you're both on the same wavelength.

- *"Off the record."* To some journalists, this means that the information will not appear in the story. Others interpret it to mean that the information can be used but that it must be attributed to an "industry source" or "industry observer," so that the real source cannot be identified.
- *"Not for attribution."* The material will be used, but neither the speaker nor his or her company will be identified. The speaker's industry will be identified.
- *"For background."* Similar to "not for attribution." The industry will be identified, but not the company or the source. For either of these terms, however, the journalist may ask if it's all right to identify the company.
- *"On deep background."* The meaning of this term is as murky as the true identity of Watergate's famed "Deep Throat." It can mean any of three very different things:

  1. The information is strictly to aid the journalist's understanding of the subject and is not to be used as a part of the story.
  2. The information may be used providing there is no attribution of any kind. For example: "The News has learned that . . . ," giving the impression that the journalist is the source.
  3. The information may be attributed to a source who,

like "Deep Throat," is not identified even by industry, but might—with the source's agreement—be identified by type of position ("a high level executive").

Caution: Unless you know the interviewer and have developed a relationship based on mutual trust, never say anything you do not want attributed to you, regardless of the terminology the interviewer uses when requesting the interview.

Preparing your answers

Once you know the topic or the focus, you can begin to plan your presentation. Whether you're to be interviewed on the air or for print, it's important to be very specific and very precise about what you want to say and how you want to say it. In either situation, the time pressures will be such that if you ramble or stray, you'll lose.

First, list the five points that you particularly want to convey—or the five questions you would most like to be asked. Arrange them in order of importance to you, not the interviewer.

Next, list the five questions you'd least like to be asked. Now, write out answers to the questions on *both* lists, using the guidelines that follow.

Recommendation: If the interviewer has given you an advance list of questions, do prepare answers to them. But don't limit yourself to that list if it does not include the major ideas you want to get across. (We'll tell you in Chapter 9 how to get those points across even if the interviewer doesn't ask about them.) Don't expect the interviewer to adhere strictly to the list, either. He or she may develop other points later, and is unlikely to call you back with periodic updates. Or he or she may simply have given you only the major questions, not the sub-questions.

Keep your answers as simple and to-the-point as possible. Radio and TV allot airtime down to the split second, so you'll be speaking within a very rigid time frame. "Two minutes" means exactly that. There is no leeway. Even a "half hour" program doesn't allow thirty minutes for speaking; commercials, introductions, and other interruptions significantly reduce the time available. Therefore, you have to be prepared to deliver the essence of an entire speech in relatively few words, leaving out nuances and backup points.

On TV, where time is especially tight, the preference is often for answers no more than sixty seconds long. You can speak about 140 words in that time.

Start, then, by developing 140-word answers to your ten questions. Put your main point into your first sentence, in case that's all you have a chance to say. But do prepare material to augment those answers. You want to be sure you can answer each of the interviewer's questions with a bright, short reply—as well as a more in-depth response, should you be given the opportunity for one.

Once you have given your basic answer, says Yate, you can buy yourself a little more time by asking, "May I give you an example?" The interviewer isn't likely to cut you off—unless he or she absolutely must—for fear of seeming rude.

"Just be sure your example is punchy and short," Yate advises.

To be believable, be specific. "Vague answers suggest

that you can't back up your information," says Carol Jaber. "Give concrete examples. Use statistics or dollar figures." And talk about individuals, rather than entities. The public will be more favorably impressed if you say, "Bob Jones, our environmental supervisor, has been making great strides in that area. . . ." than if you say, "Our Compliance Department maintains the highest standards. . . ."

If you are being taped, you may think that you don't have to be as careful, because the tape can be stopped if you make an error, and you can speak again. But that is a risky line of thinking. Tapes are also edited, and time constraints and the show host's point of view will be the primary considerations in any editing that's done. When you present your ideas concisely, there's less likelihood that they can be twisted—either purposely or accidentally—when taken out of context.

When being interviewed by a print journalist, ask how long the interview will take. This will give you an idea of how detailed the interviewer wants your answers to be. It will also help ensure that you get your most important points across before your time runs out.

Recommendation: Read the day's newspapers and listen to a news program before you are interviewed, no matter how early in the day your interview is scheduled. This will help keep you from being surprised by a question that may have come up within the last few hours, or by an interviewer's reference to a recent event.

How to rehearse

With media interviews, as with job interviews, it's important to rehearse your answers until you know them so thoroughly, and are so comfortable with them, that you can deliver them smoothly and believably. Stumbling through a job interview can cost you the job, but stumbling through a media interview can cost you your credibility.

Just thinking through your answers after you've written them out is not enough, says Rosen. "It's important to see if you can say them out loud."

For an even more valid test, he says, "We recommend that people get together with others in their area of expertise and have them ask the questions." The reason, he explains, is that such people are generally more well versed in the subject than the journalist will be, and can therefore ask more pointed questions.

Recommendation: Be sure to ask them to be tough on you. Otherwise they may pull their punches. You want them to help you prepare for anything you may come up against.

Another effective technique, he says, is to videotape or audiotape your answers and then see if your peers find them believable. Video also helps you to see if you look calm or tense, and whether or not your gestures are distracting or off-putting. (For more on body language, see Chapter 9.)

Practice until you can give each of your answers unhesitatingly and speak in a smooth, conversational style. "People talk with the interviewers the way they write cover letters for job applications," remarks Yate, who has had experience with both. You want to avoid the common failing of being overly formal. It not only makes you sound stilted, it makes you less credible. Why? You appear to be afraid to deviate from a prepared text. Practice until you sound spontaneous.

Observation: Preparing for a radio interview or an

interview with a print journalist is somewhat simpler than preparing for a TV interview. The reason: You can look at your notes on occasion, if necessary. On TV, however, do not refer to notes for anything other than statistics that you could not reasonably be expected to remember. You want to present yourself as a person who is knowledgeable and is expressing his or her own ideas, not what he or she has been told to say.

What to wear

The basic guideline when you're choosing your clothing for a TV appearance is to dress conservatively so that the audience's attention is focused on what you're saying, rather than what you're wearing. Here are some specific recommendations:

- *Wear familiar clothing,* something that you've had for a while and feel comfortable in. This is not the occasion for rushing out and buying an outfit that will present the "new you."
- *Wear lightweight clothing:* TV lights are hot. If you're being interviewed in the dead of winter, carry light clothing with you and change at the studio, Rosen suggests.
- *Avoid bold patterns, stripes, or plaids,* Rosen cautions. "They can play havoc with the video, and it will look as though there's movement in the pattern." Also avoid white—which reflects light—and black, which absorbs it. Light blues or grays are better.
- *If you wear eyeglasses,* but feel comfortable talking to others without them, leave them off; they may hide your eyes. But keep them on if you see poorly without

them. Otherwise, you may squint or appear strained or unfocused.

- *Avoid heavy jewelry* that can reflect light or clink against the microphone. The latter is a consideration for radio broadcasts, too.
- *Get an expert's advice on makeup*—what to wear and how to wear it. *Both women and men should consider powder.* For instance, if you have a receding hairline or thinning hair, powdering your forehead or bald spot will prevent a distracting shine. It will also lessen the effect of the hot lights, which may make you perspire. Perspiration can make you appear nervous or frightened—thus weakening your credibility.

What if you're going to be photographed for an article? Dress conservatively and, again, wear familiar and comfortable clothing. White shirts are fine for photos, if they're your preference. Whatever you choose, be sure that your clothing and accessories enhance your professional image.

You're now ready to use the media interview to your best advantage. Chapter 9 will suggest how.

9

How to Succeed in Media Interviews

There are two guidelines you must follow if the media interview is to be a successful experience for you:

- Put every effort into achieving your own agenda—otherwise, why are you there?
- Try not to derail the interviewer's agenda—or you may find yourself locked in battle.

Following both of those guidelines simultaneously requires a blend of determination and diplomacy. But if you've achieved a measure of success in your profession, no doubt you already possess those skills. The interview is another chance to hone them.

Communicate your key points first

When you prepared for the interview, you arranged your topics in order of importance to you. You must communicate at least the first of those topics (try for more, of course); otherwise, you have totally lost your opportunity.

Rosen voices succinctly and unarguably the technique for getting your key point across: "Lead with the lead." Otherwise, it may end up on the cutting room floor. As he explains, "Tape is edited in a top-down process. As the tape is played, the editors listen for the first good cut. Once they find that, they may never go beyond it. In print, it's just the opposite. When there is too much material, it's edited from the bottom up."

As you can see, even though the procedures are reversed, the effect is the same: The good material near the beginning is what always survives.

You can present your key point first, regardless of what question is asked. But don't just sit there hoping for the right questions. Plan to use a technique called "bridging" to lead from the interviewer's question to the point you wish to make.

Examples: "Before we get to that, let me fill you in on . . ."

"I think that would be clearer if I explained——first."

"That's a good question. Interestingly enough, people often ask me [at which point you state the question you want to answer]."

Remember, though, the caution against derailing the interviewer's agenda. So position your answer as something that will be informative and helpful, keep your tone upbeat, and forge ahead. If the interviewer protests, "You haven't answered my question," and then repeats it, you can answer it now—you've said what you wanted to say.

Repeat this procedure as often as you need to. If the interviewer has given you an accurate idea of what the focus will be, and you have prepared accordingly, the interview should not degenerate into a tug of war. If it does, or threatens to, simply say in a calm voice: "This is not what you asked me to talk about with you and I'm not prepared to discuss it." Make an effort to sound as pleasant as possible. You want the audience on your side.

Observation: You'll find bridging statements useful, too, for handling questions you simply don't want to answer. Says Jaber, "Respond with 'I'm glad you asked me that'—and then answer whatever you want to."

Answering the killer questions

You can't use bridging indefinitely to avoid troublesome questions, however. Some questions that are designed to put you on the spot require that you defend yourself. If that happens, try this three-step technique that Rosen suggests for turning negatives into positives:

- *Defuse the negative.* Give a response such as "I would not characterize it that way" or "I don't agree with your choice of words." But do not repeat the allegation with which you disagree. If you do, the audience, or readers, will hear, or see, those damning words coming from you, and will continue to make the association, despite your denial.

  Example: What more vivid example is there than

former President Richard Nixon's statement "I am not a crook." The whole world remembers the statement, but somehow has overlooked the word "not" that Nixon inserted into it.

Example: When New York City Mayor David Dinkins responded to criticism of the city after a rash of killings, *USA Today* ran his denial as a headline for the whole country to see, and remember: 'This is not Dodge City.' A full five months later, *The New York Times* followed up with a news item pointing out that New York City indeed was "not Dodge City": New York reported more than two thousand homicides in 1990; Dodge City reported none.

- *Answer the question.* You have an answer ready, because this is one of the five questions that you don't want to be asked. "If you don't answer it, the reporter will say so," Rosen warns. "But if you genuinely can't answer it, give as good a reason as possible. For example, 'It's in litigation.'"
- *Make your own point.* Now build your bridge, says Rosen, with words such as "And along those lines, you might be interested to know that . . ." And make whichever of your top five points you have not yet communicated.

In addition to the allegations to which you must respond, be alert to other types of questions and situations that can cause difficulty:

- *Insulting questions.* You do not have to answer these at all; you are entitled to be treated with respect. Say simply, "I will not respond to anything that absurd, so let's get back to the issues."
- *Questions that reveal basic misconceptions.* Don't

allow misconceptions to go unchecked. If the interviewer asks a question or makes a statement that shows some lack of understanding, make a brief correction quickly, without being condescending or didactic. Bear in mind that if a second question is based on an assumption that you did not correct in the previous question, it is clumsy for you to go back to correct your previous answer. It also implies that you are manipulating both the interviewer and the public.

- *Recommendation:* If you understand the interviewer's style, or have watched or listened to a number of interview programs, you may be able to anticipate a troublesome question. Yate suggests taking the offensive with a question of your own: "What question are you leading up to?"

- *Putting down put-downs.* If the interviewer or another guest corrects you on a point that you should know, and do know, try responding with "Thank you for that," and keep right on going. Use a light, even breezy, tone that's not snide, but that suggests that the other person's implication that you are uninformed only reveals his or her ignorance.

At this point, you may be wondering why we're offering all these tips for handling troublesome questions if the media interview is such an "opportunity." The reason is simply that the difficult encounters, although less common, require more forethought and preparation on your part.

Special tips for TV

When you're being interviewed on television, the way you "come across" is important. If there's anything distracting or unconvincing about your demeanor, your message may be lost.

- **Watch your eyes.** Learn to ignore everything—the bright lights, the glare, the people—and concentrate on what the host or the interviewer is saying. Keep that focus at all times. Try not to lower your eyes when you answer a question; you'll appear evasive. And avoid rolling them upward while thinking through a point, Rosen cautions: "You don't know when they'll do a tight shot [a close-up], and if you appear to be looking heavenward for help, that will do nothing for your credibility."
- **Use your hands.** If you normally use hand gestures when you speak, use them during the interview. It's a good way to release nervous energy. But avoid any light, fluttery gestures that could make you appear ineffectual. If you don't usually gesture, don't try to force it—it will *look* forced. Instead, just let your hands rest in your lap.
- **Remember that you're always "on."** As long as the program is being broadcast, the cameras are rolling. Monitor your body language whether you are speaking or simply sitting there listening. You can never be sure whether the camera is focused in on a revealing tight shot of your face or a long shot that could show you fidgeting in your seat.

Special tips for radio

Radio presentations are a challenge even to an experienced speaker, because it's not just the audience that's invisible. So are you. Your voice alone must gain and hold audience attention. It must also convey your personality and credibility.

To be successful on radio, speak in a sincere, straightforward manner and with a clear voice. Also:

- **Stay as relaxed as possible.** When you're nervous, your voice may become higher pitched or sound strained.
- **Speak with your usual volume.** Don't try to talk too loudly. Tone, rather than volume, makes points on radio. But do try to talk in a slightly lower tone if you can do so without straining; a lower voice sounds more authoritative.
- **Move around as little as possible.** It can affect your vocal sound.
- **Avoid making distracting noises,** such as coughing, throat clearing, sneezing, drumming your fingers, moving your feet, or playing with papers. The microphone picks up such sounds.

Recommendation: For both TV and radio interviews, avoid verbal signals that suggest subordination or insecurity, such as an upward inflection that turns statements into questions, or qualifying what you say with "I think" or "sort of" or "just."

Special tips for working with print journalists

You are probably more likely to be interviewed by print journalists than by broadcast journalists. There's a vast number of specialized trade and industry magazines constantly seeking new stories and new angles. You are also more likely to develop a continuing relationship with print journalists. Here's how to make those relationships harmonious:

- *Be candid and cooperative.* When journalists come to you with questions, answer them as completely and honestly as possible. Don't lie. Be straightforward about admitting errors. (Again, don't lie.) If you aren't honest, there's bound to be another source out there who'll gladly point a finger—perhaps a disgruntled former employee. If the journalist doesn't find that person, you're likely to find your fudging revealed later in the "Letters to the Editor" column—where people who didn't even read the article will read that you lied.

- *Respect deadlines.* Don't wait until a half hour before press time to call a reporter with big news. If something major is going to break close to deadline, advise the journalist ahead of time so he or she can be prepared. And when a journalist on deadline calls you for information, it's to your advantage to get the answers fast, even if you must disrupt your own schedule. You won't have any input once the deadline passes.

- *Realize that journalists don't work for you.* Unlike your public relations counselor, they do not put your interests first. Their first concern is an accurate story, and they do not need your permission or approval to print it.

- *They will work with you, however.* They will accommodate you, within the limits of professionalism, if you treat them with respect. To demand "Don't print that!" is to guarantee that it will be printed. But if you ask, "How are you planning to use thus-and-such information?" or say, "I'm really not comfortable with thus-

and-such" during an interview when you've been cooperative, you may very well find that you can retract something you wish you hadn't said—unless it's central to the story.

- *Speak for yourself.* Don't let your public relations counselor speak for you during an interview. The days of the mouthpiece who covers for the boss by saying, "What Mr. Jones means to say is . . ." are over. He or she can help you prepare for the interview, of course. But a good public relations counselor will know when to sit in on an interview and when to introduce you to the journalist and then leave. In fact, most editors and reporters refuse to permit a public relations counselor to sit in. If there are loose ends to tie up after the interview, or extra information you promised to obtain, your counselor can step in then. Otherwise, he or she should stay out of it.

- *Again, remember that you're always "on."* The entire time that you spend with the journalist is part of the interview. Even if he or she is using a tape recorder— which is fairly common—the interview begins before the machine is turned on and continues after it is turned off.

- *Offer to help—but not interfere—with the final story.* Few publications permit review of a story before it goes to press. But no journalist wants to misquote or misrepresent a subject. If you ask journalists to verify quotes or numbers once the story is complete, they may very well agree. And they will certainly appreciate your making yourself available to clarify points.

  Caution: If you imply that the story might otherwise contain errors, the offended journalist will probably check nothing in the completed story with you.

A professional, well-organized interviewer for any of the media will give you a chance to make one final remark or add one wrap-up point: "Thank you for your time, Mr. Expert. Before we close, do you have anything you'd like to add?" or "Is there anything we've missed?" Be ready to put forth whatever point you haven't had a chance to cover, or to re-emphasize your main point if you've been able to cover them all. This is yet another opportunity for you to benefit from your interview.

10

Crisis Interviews

There may come a time when you're suddenly facing journalists and trying to explain a major problem. Why, for example, did one of your company's chemical tanks release a small amount of poisonous gas into the atmosphere? Why is your company closing a plant that employs a large number of people in your community?

This time, *all* the questions the journalists ask will be the ones you don't want to answer. But the worst thing you can do is lie. The next worst thing is to issue an opinion based on skimpy information in the hope that you'll later be proved right by the facts.

Observation: If you are the best source, make yourself available even though it is the last thing you want to do. For one thing, if you don't, the press may be resentful, and that can work against you. For another, it's their job to get the story. If they can't get it from you, they'll have to get it from someone else, who may not be as well informed, may not have your best interests at heart, and may even have an ax to grind.

Anticipate and prepare

What you can, and must, do is anticipate the questions, prepare your answers—and also prepare the points that you want to convey, whether you're asked or not. Here are some of the kinds of questions you can expect.

The "either-or" question
Example: "Either your company wants to keep the citizens of this town employed, or it wants to close down the factory. Which is it?"

This is an attempt to distort the issues and paint you into a corner. Your best defense is to point out that the "either-or" case is spurious. Try the defusing technique—"I would not make the distinction that way." Then bridge to the issues that confront your company at this time.

The "multiple choice" question
Example: "Will you replace outmoded equipment to meet new EPA guidelines, repair the old equipment, or just shut it down temporarily?"

Just because the journalist is supplying the answers doesn't mean that you can't ignore them and supply one of your own.

The "number one priority" question
Example: "What is your company's number one priority in fighting pollution?"

If you say that it is reducing your plant's output of

airborne pollutants, you may be attacked for ignoring water purity restrictions. Your best defense is to say, "We are attacking many major concerns, including . . ."

The "off the record" question
Example: "Off the record, what do you think the cost of the cleanup will be?"

Always respond as though your statements will become a matter of public record. Odds are, they will.

The "second guess" question
Example: "How do you think your competitors will respond to your new product line?"

Try, "You'd better ask them that question."

The "statement" question
Example: "You obviously don't want to spend money on community developments."

Again, defuse. Do not say, "I wouldn't say that we don't want to spend money on community developments." Rather, "I don't agree with your choice of words." Then, convert the journalist's statement into a question that you want to answer: "If you're asking about our current programs, let me explain them for you."

The "yes or no" question
Example: "Did your company take adequate safety precautions? Yes or no?"

This is an overt ploy to make you look bad, and it will work. To limit the damage, say, "We will be issuing that information shortly." But don't pick an arbitrary date when an answer will be forthcoming.

The "what if" question
Example: "What if fatalities result—will your firm make restitution to the families of the victims?"

Don't let yourself get pulled into a series of speculations. Journalists can trap you in a seemingly unimportant one and then lead you into more damaging statements.

The "policy statement" question
This can occur when you go before the media armed with information on a specific issue. Then a journalist asks about a general issue related to the matter you came to talk about.

Example: "What is your stand on the environment?" (When you were asked to discuss your company's new water-pollution control effort.)

To avoid a lengthy silence or an ill-conceived reply, use a bridging statement to tie your answer into the matter you are *prepared* to discuss: "As we have demonstrated by our handling of this current problem . . ." Then point to the specifics of what you are doing about the current problem as an example of your company's outlook on the general issue.

Observation: Policy questions present a golden opportunity to display your background research and tell of past company or community activities that show your firm in a positive way.

The scene counts. If you're at the scene of a problem situation—a strike, environmental problem, etc.—don't allow the interview to take place with that scene in the background. Instead, stand away from the scene to avoid reinforcing the image of your company's association with the problem.